Dancing The Digital Tune

© 2014 by Manish Grover

Title: Dancing The Digital Tune
Subtitle: The 5 Principles of Competing in a Digital World
Date: 02 Nov 2014

e-Book ISBN: 978-0-692-32176-8
Softcover ISBN: 978-0-692-35874-0
Hardcover ISBN: 978-0-692-32175-1

Author: Manish Grover
Publisher: CD Press, www.CompetingInDigital.com
Title: Rakesh Prasad
Cover page design: Achraf Elkaami
Editing assistance: Dina Petrosky, Smart Connections PR, Veena Grover
Marketing & PR assistance: Joanne Hogue & Dina Petrosky, Smart Connections PR

Working space: Dunkin' Donuts, Panera, and Starbucks. Richard Martinez at Dunkin' Donuts is one team leader who is excellently applying The Principle of Customer Interaction.

Keeping me humble & motivated: Saritha and Arya Grover

Dancing The Digital Tune

The 5 Principles of Competing in a Digital World

Manish Grover

This book is dedicated to my parents

About the Author

I could say that I am a strategist, marketer, manager, leader or consultant, but that would exclude my other identities of father, son, engineer, consumer, student, blogger, coach, biker, musician (aspiring), chef (decent) and among many others, a dreamer.

Should I choose a professional label, or a personal one? It depends on the context, I guess. So I'll leave it to you.

The 5 principles in this book have come from my experience consulting with global brand organizations over almost two decades. I've helped launch multi-country initiatives with significant impact and devised long term business-technology roadmaps. I've created value propositions that emphasize solutions for our customers' most pressing problems.

I'm also a marketer and buyer of products and services. I've sold and been sold to. I've learned what works and what doesn't. I've created and executed razor sharp campaigns based on these five principles.

Enjoy the book. It's my view of the future of customer engagement.

Manish Grover

MBA (Carnegie Mellon) | MS (Florida Atlantic) | BE Honors (BITS Pilani)

Twitter: *@manishgrover*

www.manishgrover.com

Dancing The Digital Tune

The 5 Principles of Competing in a Digital World

This book presents an overarching and systematic process to create our digital strategy in today's social and connected world. In a rapidly evolving and connected digital world, traditional digital engagement models will be inadequate for future successes.

We need an approach that orients our organizations to the new connected world. The 5 actionable frameworks in this book will help us align our digital strategy with the customer. This book is about partnership with customers, about connecting with them on multiple levels, about crafting uniqueness, about leveraging the transformation this connected world is going through, and as a result, about staying ahead of the pack.

Learn why and how we should:

- Not leave to chance what customers need to build context
- Unify emotional appeal with physical interactions
- Be un-commoditized
- Not act as the proverbial 5 blind men while engaging with customers
- Look beyond and create a chain of links

The unique perspective that the 5 principles provide will help us connect our digital strategy with broader organizational goals, industry dynamics and above all, with our customers. The 5 principles represent a trophy. Those who will rise above the pack in today's connected world will win.

Contents

Acknowledgements

I'm grateful to all the amazing people who bring innovations to the world every day. Collectively, and individually among our multiple personas, we are our own best source of learning about what is to be done, how is it to be done, and how to improve what is being done.

Before We Start

If you would like to receive new material as it becomes available, please visit *www.CompetingInDigital.com/DancingTheDigitalTune* to enter your email address.

Or scan the QR code to go to the site on your phone.

Background and Important Guidelines

The intent of this book is to help us think in a systematic way about engaging in a world where business models are being transformed by the digital revolution.

It is critical to revisit and evolve how we engage with customers, and how we build an ecosystem that brings the full power of what we have to offer to our customers. Businesses are not operating in isolation today. In fact, the traditional definition of how we went to market just a few years ago is under siege. Businesses that were considered partners are rapidly becoming competitors. It's a frantic race to secure the top spot in our customers' minds. No longer is it enough to be an efficient, well-oiled machine delivering to fulfill the demand, because the very sources of that demand are being disrupted. Customers are being provided so many options that only those who will earn a trusted position in their minds, and those who embed themselves into the customers decision cycles will thrive. This automatically implies that we review and transform how we look at the market.

I've organized this book into five principles that will help us do exactly that. These five principles make up the foundational framework for a strategic analysis of this new era of business ecosystems. The principles will also help us identify a plan and define an execution roadmap. As we progress, we'll unravel and reveal each of these five principles. The principles don't necessarily have to be followed in the order presented, but it was a reasonably logical way for me to organize this book, and my thought process around the building blocks.

Let's begin by thinking of some very emotionally strong connections. When was the last time we posed for a lasting Kodak Moment? Or heard the melodious Nokia ring tone? These were such successful advertising campaigns that we still feel nostalgic about them. I wanted to start with this so it sets us up to sit up and question everything.

Companies often stumble upon the next big thing, and many of them fail to capitalize on the opportunities. Responding quickly and effectively to changes in the marketplace is critical today. The most important trends in the marketplace start out as whispers, and grow so rapidly that by the time we convince ourselves that something needs to be done, it's too late.

Denial leads to inertia, and inertia leads to extinction.

Embracing a systematic way to think about customer engagement and building intimacy is vital.

My intent is to provide a yardstick that is convenient enough for us to assess your operations rapidly while also decoding the actions we must take to plug the gaps. The five principles are based on a simple premise that the world is connected – mobile, contextual, social, aware, fast acting – and the traditional methods of winning customers will be inadequate for the future.

It's obvious. Thinking about customer engagement comes before thinking about our innovation pipeline. Customer engagement is no longer a way to think about engaging customers with our products and services. Instead it's really about determining which new products and services to launch in order to engage our customers and target market. It's also true that the target markets are changing rapidly, so it's even more important to constantly think about customer engagement first.

- Did Google start with the vision of one day providing mobile phones and Google Glass?
- Did Amazon begin its journey knowing that it would be the digital media distribution powerhouse it is today?

- Did Facebook start out with aim of being the social powerhouse it is today?

In all these cases the target markets and their characteristics were changing. And the companies evolved to almost transform what they already had in their products portfolio. One could even argue that these firms changed the way the market was used to evolving.

At this point, I'd like to insert a word of caution for the purposes of this book. While examples such as the above – and the many that I'll refer to throughout the book - serve to illustrate the point being discussed, they also limit our learning if we identify too closely with them. They cloud our ability to analyze and apply to our particular situation. They tend to idolize certain aspects while glossing over the many shortcomings. They inspire but they don't guide. They are not necessarily a statement of intent. They tend to muddy the notion of best practices. And they provide the potently obvious but probably false idea that some firms really had a strategy or intended to do what they did. A lot of outcomes we often speak of - and quote - came about without being designed as such. Indeed some visionaries may have everything planned out when they started, but I believe they are an exception, not the rule.

I designed the frameworks in this book to help us analyze a situation from our own perspective while keeping in mind the broader ecosystem dynamics. The frameworks are a tool for us to design our strategic response. While explaining the frameworks, I will consider some examples to refine the concepts and begin to make an implementation plan. Examples do keep things interesting. Many may indeed be relevant and factual. But I'll strongly recommend and focus on analyzing the concepts first. Let's think of the examples in this book as a way for us to get a sense of the outcomes, to see for ourselves what can be done better, and as a way to validate that we are on the right track.

It's like they say:

"To become successful, think about what successful people did before they became successful, instead of how they behave after they are successful."

Or something like that. I know you get the point. Agree and nod your head, or shake your head and disagree. All I want is to encourage you to take a stand. I want to change the world, and I hope you do, too.

Let's dig right in.

Evolving Towards the New Definition of Channels

The digital economy is disrupting many time honored business models. It's impossible to sit back and enjoy the ride anymore.

Let's start with a few outcomes we've seen in the past several years. We will never know how systematically these outcomes were realized. Was this evolution planned out when these journeys began? Or was it that as the path lit up, the vision cleared and the future was molded? Regardless, as we have seen with the explosion of innovation in 2014, the winds of change are blowing stronger than ever, and they promise to become even more prevalent.

Premium for the Excitement of World Domination

In 2009, heavily in debt, and yet looking to utilize my new found knowledge of finance gained at Carnegie Mellon, I was looking to invest what little money I had. Like most small time investors I was risk averse, and everyone said that Amazon stock was overpriced. My gut feeling said that Amazon was doing everything right. The customers loved it – I know I did - or at least they checked out Amazon first, sometimes even before Google. Amazon was leveraging its capabilities well to make forays into new areas. However everyone quoted the low profit margins and warned about the quickly heating competitive landscape. I let the left side of my brain get the better of the right side and held off.

Now, see where Amazon is today. It's obvious that had I listened to the right side of my brain, I could have made a very handsome profit. Amazon's stock price shot through the roof and only recently after troubles with their new "Fire" smartphone and a weaker holiday season fell by 10%.

I just wish that I had invested when it was at $90 instead of listening to pundits on how overpriced the stock was. What was going on here? We all know profits have been measly, so this can't be about just making money. What are the investors seeing? Are they seeing a future where Amazon becomes the hub of commerce?

Let's break it down:

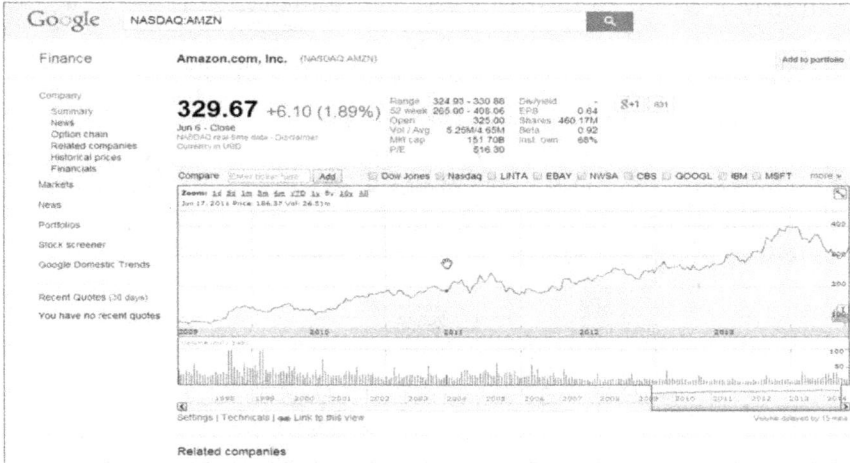

- Amazon Prime is the loyalty platform on which Amazon is building the functional blocks of its ecosystem
- Amazon Kindle is building a digital media ecosystem
- Amazon Publishing is helping people achieve their dreams and usurping the traditional rules of the publishing industry.
- Amazon has moved from being simply a retail store to being positioned as an alternative to Netflix, or even cable.
- Amazon has become a cloud provider and is fast becoming the first choice for many enterprise businesses in addition to companies and entrepreneurs just starting out.
- Amazon is a thriving market place for all kinds of sellers making Amazon the one place to find everything you may want
- Amazon is getting into our daily lives with grocery shopping
- Amazon is making delivery easy and will open up exciting new models for retail

It looks like every capability feeds into each other as the online super market – if we can even call it that - goes from strength to strength. Customers can't do without Amazon. Nothing seems out of reach. Now let's take a look at one of the most revered brand organizations of all time.

The P&G brands are an integral part of our life.

- We can't do without these products.
- We swear by them.
- The ROE (return on equity) indicates shareholder return is about 5 times of that of Amazon.
- Competition is hot but the brands are firmly entrenched.

The stock price in the past 10 years has risen by approximately 20% while Amazon's stock price grew 400%.

That's a massive difference. Why? Could it be the difference between the known, and the excitement of the unknown – the difference between a business that is predictable and one that is riding the waves of innovation to make itself relevant, anticipating world domination.

As Amazon rapidly innovates to match the momentum of a connected world, what would we do if we were at Amazon? Or at P&G? Would we continue to expand, disrupt, pull back, consolidate, or stabilize? In this digital world, the future is unpredictable, but only if we stop innovating and building on our core promise.

Evolution Towards the Purpose: Nike. Shoes? Sports? Fitness?

After all is said and done, is Nike a shoe and apparel maker? That phrase grates on my mind and seems completely wrong. Because what Nike has done is push the boundaries of where their products play.

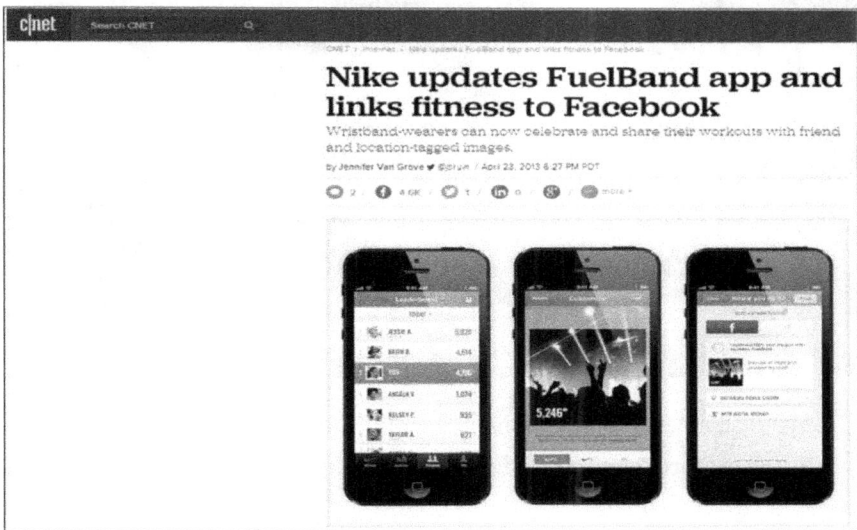

They've taken the word fitness and made it their own. Fitness is more social and more stylish than ever before. The physical means to achieve that goal are almost invisible, except there being a strong underlying thread of aspiration supported by a reliable physical form. Nike progressed from being a supplier of equipment to being a facilitator of activities. Now it is moving beyond that to building a community of zealots. These zealots are also powerful brand ambassadors, almost without knowing that they are.

Nike has now embedded itself into the daily ecosystem of its customers. It has the capability to wake us up, stop us from gluttony, and ask us to cheer on a friend running a grueling marathon. Could Nike's next partnership be with fitness centers, organic food makers, or with doctors and nutritionists? Will it help us buy the right foods, and just as a GPS does, help us get back on track?

The Pursuit of Dreams: The Harley-Davidson Owners Group

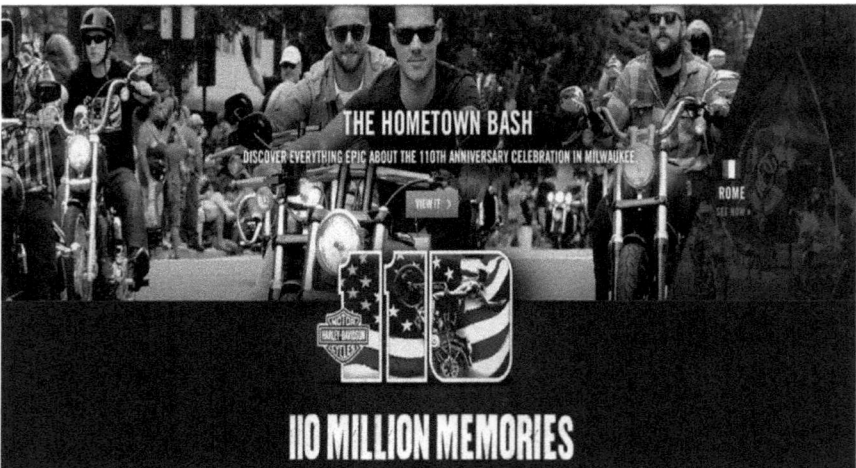

Riding a Harley-Davidson is a way of life for those that own the brand of motorcycle. The Harley-Davidson brand enjoys passionate user loyalty. They've combined the physical attraction of their product with a powerful emotional attachment that expands beyond geographical boundaries. The characteristics of their product cover more than raw physical performance, making the possession of it linked to many intangibles. And in doing so, they are bringing so many different factors together, in turn allowing their users to constantly add to the value of their ecosystem. All that's needed is a little careful nurturing.

Take a look at how Harley Davidson promotes riding their brand of motorcycle as our must-do activity; helping us begin to "really live life". When we realize we've completely missed living our life, what's a very feasible redemption? Buy a Harley! It's a dream people look forward to. And Harley-Davidson is doing all it can to keep the dream of riding unfettered on the open road alive. It's a complex mix of inspiration, uniqueness, belonging, pride, accomplishment and passion, almost to the point of being fanatic.

Harley-Davidson is not alone in building a fervent community; it's just one of the more quoted. Indeed Honda and Yamaha are not far behind in sales and aficionados. Understanding what kind of motorcycle people want amounts to a table stakes game. Building a network of activities and partners who help customers meet their dreams is what's ultimately making the difference. The dream is what matters, not the motorcycle.

An Exciting and Nervously Scary Proposition: The Connected Home

And we come to the Internet of Things. Every device is now capable of transmitting and receiving information.

Your doctor can now receive real time reports about your blood pressure and exercise levels so she can take preventative actions immediately. Your refrigerator is likely going to be ordering your groceries for you. The television may automatically turn on and switch to your favorite show as it detects you walking into the door, and your oven may set itself to preheat based on the recipes you have on for that day. These are exciting possibilities. For businesses, your equipment in the field will automatically call for service, and customers won't have to worry about keeping up with their warranties (if that's not your very business model).

Even as everyone is speaking about data privacy and machines taking over the world, the Internet of Things or IoT is the one thing that's going to make our business proposition as contextual and as targeted as it can get.

The biggest strategic risk is not security or privacy. It's us, the architects of business, failing to think of how we're going to play in this ecosystem. Are we going to be able to design a strategic response to this trend, or fall behind as our competitors secure that position in our customers' minds?

What can P&G do, what can Harley do, what can Amazon do, what can Home Depot do, and how do they do it so they incrementally build an interconnected network of partners? Can our next home improvement project be forecasted by the devices in our home and planned by Facebook?

The successes of the traditional model of customer engagement will not form the basis for continued success. The traditional model tries to decipher how a business can target customers better and sell to them as a single firm, often competing against the rest of the world. That model divides you into brands and products.

Until it comes to a grinding and sudden halt that is. I don't have to mention the spectacular failures of some really spectacular companies in recent years because I am sure those names are already flashing through your mind.

The fundamental concept we'll address through the five principles in this book is that the digital economy is not only eliminating scarcity of information, it's also bringing businesses together. And in the process this revolution is rendering some businesses redundant because they are not in the right customer experience path. That simply implies that customers have several paths available they can choose from to arrive at the same result. And unless businesses learn to play well and help each other, and in the process help their customers, they'll lose the race.

- Will an Amazon drone grocery offering help if the customer is ordering groceries from the console of their treadmill and their neighborhood Boy Scouts are delivering it? It has the potential to, but only when we stop thinking of delivery and start thinking of dreams, and communities, and how people want to cultivate them.
- Will a mobile payments app save a bank if the restaurant splits the payments among friends right at the table using mechanisms such as Target's REDcard?
- A technology provider selling multi-million dollar contracts will fail to engage if there is not a good match with the client whose business it wants to power. Throw in the client's other business process partners who must be integrated, and things get complex

pretty quickly. What will it take to be in the path of vision of our customers, or even help build it for them?

The definition of "channel" is evolving to mean a set of interacting businesses working together to meet customers' needs, not just as a means of product sales, service and distribution of a single firm. Customer engagement is becoming an assessment of the entire needs spectrum and the means being used to fulfill the needs. If the channel or medium – as per our new definition – attempts to take advantage of customers by seeming to lock them in, or does not offer them the education they need, customers will switch to another channel – which implies they'll move their business to a different set of companies that make up that other channel. And because the digital world is eliminating barriers to information and access, customers will ultimately decide which companies and products make up a preferred channel. The gap in traditional customer engagement models will fuel the next wave of disruption. The only way to survive will be to build an ecosystem that will help us look at our products from the customer's eyes, and do business with everyone who engages with the customer.

In fact, the most business-friendly social networks for the next generation may not be the online platforms we use today, but the communities based on motivations and dreams. Think of the physical network as Facebook, and the social network as Harley-Davidson.

The Five Principles – Engaging with Customers as People, not Users

"Today's buyer has the tools to be able to connect the dots and derive inter-linkages, even if we don't want them to."

– Manish Grover

(or insert your name here because you could have said it too)

In any system, complex or simple, a set of people and processes come together to achieve results, desired or otherwise. An ecosystem is made up of the interacting people, their needs and the products and services they use. For our purposes, we will define an ecosystem from the perspective of the customer looking at us. And we will attempt to decode the entire spectrum of customer needs which extends much beyond our own products and services.

The biggest surprise for all of us is this: how we would like to meet a specific need is not relevant in today's world. We must engage with customers as people. When we stop thinking of customers as buyers of our products but as just people with many different needs and motivations, then we will fully leverage the ecosystem that awaits us with open arms. Counter-intuitive as it may have seemed until just a few years ago, this approach is imperative to follow in today's modern, connected and contextual world. Today's buyer has the tools to be able to connect the dots and derive inter-linkages, even if we don't want them to.

It's surprising how a seemingly common definition is so difficult to understand when it comes to defining the future of our own companies. We see so many definitions of the term "ecosystem," but it is always a combination of internal systems and people, or isolated issues, or a cycle of higher level processes such as acquisition and retention, or even vendor and supplier partnerships. On numerous occasions no doubt, we have all started with trying to understand the customer, but soon the customer perspective is forgotten as we try to analyze the complexity of our own internal processes, budgets and organizational dynamics. And what comes out is hardly what was intended.

In the absence of an actionable framework to achieve these goals in the new socially connected world, we have been rendered utterly helpless in the age of information abundance. What was a proven system of make-promote-sell just a few years ago is now a guessing game. If we do just that, we'll do all the right things, and we'll still spectacularly fail.

In order to build a successful business blue print, it's not enough to develop, shout about and promote products that meet isolated needs. We must be in the critical path of our customers' choice cycles. That means we must evolve our business based on our knowledge of the interactions not only across channels, but also across needs.

- Why did Google (a search and advertising firm) buy Motorola?
- Why did Salesforce.com (a CRM software firm) acquire the marketing campaigns provider ExactTarget?
- Why did Amazon (a marketplace) develop the Kindle hardware?

All of these actions are those of companies evolving with their customers. They are anticipating and tackling the most common objections and competition against their business model. If they don't, they'll probably be swept aside by the next wave of innovation.

This concept of an evolving ecosystem is important to understand and follow for both consumer oriented businesses as well as for business-business products. Once we begin to place our customers in the middle of the drawing, the right interactions will emerge.

What we need is an ecosystem as defined from our customers' vantage point, embedding ourselves in our customers' decision process, being available where they are, and being there when they need advice.

Because if we are the right fit for customers' direct needs, it makes only half the sale.

What about the other half?

How do we ensure that our product fits in with all the other products, services and associated behaviors that the customer is now buying? Here's what we do at present:

- We gloss over them and hope that they'll automatically fall in place somehow.
- We make that analysis the customer's responsibility, letting their advisors and consultants figure it out.

And we give up control to factors that we don't control. Instead, we need to actively think about that crucial other half of the equation because it defines what product we really need in order to succeed in an interconnected world. And doing it once is not enough because next time around, the situation won't be the same.

The spectrum of needs we will develop through the frameworks in this book will not only be about what the customer wants, but also about the "why" behind the need?

- Why does the customer want what we think she wants?
- What triggered the need?
- Did she try something else before?
- Where do our products and services fit in this new spectrum of needs?
- Are there any influencers? Are there any motivators?
- What could the needs of the motivators or influencers be?

Nokia and Blackberry both thought about what was going on. They reacted immediately with products that seemed to make traction. But then they stopped as the world waited with baited breath for them to respond with an answer to Apple's iPhone.

My simplistic analysis is this: First they were too late in reacting. And when they did finally react, they happened to react in the wrong way. Instead of understanding the trend, mapping it with their strengths and countering with the next best mobile platform (Android), they forgot their core value proposition. In my opinion, both should have emulated Samsung. But, instead, they tried to be Apple. That transformation was too great to pull off despite their best intentions. The fight was not at all about the best hardware device, but about customer engagement and the ecosystem that drove it. Both these companies fought the battle alone and against the rest of the world.

Some other trends we are looking at:

- Will industrial distribution be slowly supplanted by Amazon's partner and distribution network?
- Will our consumer bank be PayPal in the future, or even Apple?
- Will we need cable television?

Regardless of what we think about these and many other trends, what we need is a framework to track the changes to our customer ecosystems and craft the approach we should take.

The five principles outlined in this book will provide that missing 360 degree structure and fill in the gap between what and why. As we read through, and hopefully apply these principles and frameworks, we will discover a systematic process to build up the ecosystem for our organization. As with any innovation, implementation becomes a key early differentiator. And rapid innovation will bring with it ample opportunities for evolution. The five principles in this book will provide a validating structure for our strategies.

1. The Principle of External Reinforcement

How should we be the customers' advocate and trusted advisor, so they make a decision "with us" instead of "about us"? How could we become our customers' reference point and one of the centers of their universe? How could we become their encyclopedia or the agent that holds the key to the sea of knowledge? If customers have to look beyond us for validation, we've lost the advantage and submitted ourselves to an unforced error from our competitor (that's how I play tennis, actually). How can we embed ourselves in our customers' decision processes - explicitly or implicitly – and help them along this journey?

2. The Principle of Customer Interaction

It's a fact. Some products are high touch, some are not. Some connect at the emotional level, some at the physical interaction level, and some at both. Both engagement models peg us in our customer's mind – that peg is called our brand. But our competition is not keeping still. They are constantly trying to dethrone us through direct or flank attacks. Hence, understanding how to create relationships from both ends of the engagement spectrum is the key to success. The principle of Customer Interaction will outline the framework for us to assess the success of our customer interactions. We can then develop strategies to strengthen customer engagement and be our customers' first choice when the moments of truth arise.

3. The Principle of Un-Commoditization

Our fundamental philosophy, our passion, our excellence, these are all factors that stem from the purpose of our organization. The term "differentiation" however has become an overused technical term that seems to distance our operations from our strategy. Instead I chose to use the word un-commoditization to reflect the harsh realities of today's connected world. Without a point of un-commoditization, we can probably still survive, even grow, but will likely not thrive. This principle provides the elements of how to think about breaking away from the pack. Un-commoditization is always possible and is critical to securing a position in our customers' minds.

And it requires tremendous discipline. Without a distinctive position in the customer's mind, we might as well save our brand marketing budget.

4. The Principle of Presenting

Who are we? Like most companies, our customers can potentially use more than one of our products or services. And these products can be positioned to seamlessly complement each other. Are we presenting them in silos, or creating harmony between them? Are we meeting the portfolio of needs of our customers and potential customers in a comprehensive manner or are we content to compete by product, in silos, in the wildly tumultuous ocean for every incremental benefit we can deliver to the customer? The principle of Presenting provides a framework to think about how to move away from being a pseudo-conglomerate of business divisions and products. It is aimed at helping us become the singular brand powerhouse that we should be, striving to meet customer needs.

5. The Principle of Completion

It's obvious that our products meet a customer need. But our customers also use products which have nothing to do with us. Many of these needs are linked to each other. Contrary to traditional philosophy, these are all companies we should be working with closely. If we work together, we amplify our joint message. If we don't, we end up fighting with each other for the customers' attention. This principle is about the art of alliances, building a set of offerings that span the spectrum of customers' needs. The partnerships we choose will define us in the future. Those who are isolated will be left behind.

The five principles together enable the creation of an ecosystem. Competing in the digital economy must be about creating an ecosystem. Because only in an ecosystem will we be able to connect the dots of how our customers interact, what they need, and how our products and services fit into their worlds.

1

The Principle of External Reinforcement

The Principle of External Reinforcement is about customer partnership - it's about marketing and engaging as demanded by the new interconnected digital age. It builds towards joint decision making with customers. It's about expanding our outreach dramatically to meet unexpressed customer questions, or answers they don't expect from us.

Let's think of ourselves as customers. How do we want to engage as a customer?

1. When we want to buy something do we seek advice?
2. When we buy something and use it, do we help others in their decisions when they have a similar need?

Most people would say yes to both the above questions. It's human nature. We look for information to help us decide and we want to help others. We post reviews, read comments by others, give advice, refer each other to our favorite things, make top 10 lists, and hit the Facebook like button among a numerous other ways to express ourselves.

The Principle of External Reinforcement will help us understand how to remove the barriers to effective customer engagement by tying together information needs and stages of engagement in an overarching framework.

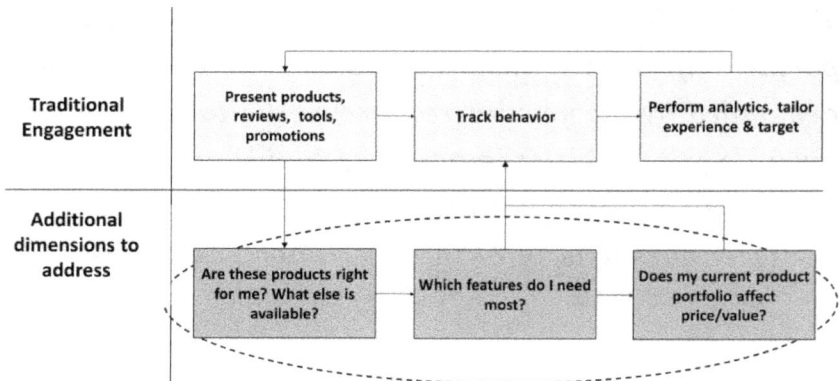

Figure 1: The natural cycle of external reinforcement

As the figure illustrates, a customer journey is only partially met when the engagement is centered on our own products and services. Customers expect that we will position ourselves in a positive light. A typical response is to cut through the clutter and go directly to the details of the service or product they are looking for. Once that is accomplished, customers will look for external reinforcement – best practices, what else is available, what they should be looking for before they decide etc. It is here that traditional engagement models fail. By focusing only on ourselves, we fail to become the reference point in the customers' minds. It is definitely desirable to be validated by external sources, but by not engaging the customer on the additional dimensions, we miss the opportunity to create a benchmark in their minds.

While we all have different ways to research and engage in conversations, satisfying this need for external reinforcement is one of the foundations of how we need to engage, sell and service in a digital world. The need for external reinforcement must be addressed at all times by engaging in a conversation not only with the customer but also with their network. By conversation I mean providing a contextual environment to better trigger and satisfy explorations by customers, noting their actions, understanding them, interpreting them, and then reacting in an appropriate manner over multiple channels and media by including their social and other networks. The Principle of External Reinforcement is about striving to understand the context of a customer's needs and buying stimuli, and by constantly acting to ensure our actions are in tune with how the customer's environment is structured, and changing.

Sources of reinforcement at every stage can often be found in advertisements, coffee table discussions, expert opinions, online reviews or even magazine articles. Customers go back and forth during their decision making. Priorities change, needs change and constraints evolve to take new forms. This is true for first time as well as repeat purchases. The kind of reinforcement customers need is dependent on:

- The stage of the purchase cycle they are in
- Whether they've been in that stage before
- Where else have they received information from? What kind?
- What are their questions?
- What assurances they are seeking before they commit?

Below are some traditional models of reinforcement. We will notice that external reinforcement is missing, or is only available as an indirect output of direct reinforcement. That is not necessarily wrong, but simply means that there is a gap in that step of the customer journey which is open to being addressed by someone else.

- Reviews by customers on products and services have always proved to an excellent tool. Businesses such as airbnb make finding accommodations easier by offering customer reviews, unit descriptions, neighborhood information and map tools to pinpoint location. The better the reviews and engagement, the better the chance of a customer going through with the transaction - once they are convinced that airbnb is the way to go.
- Amazon's recommendation engine shows what products other customers have purchased after researching the one we are currently viewing. This is a strong validation of our selection. It tries to make our job easier by making that insight available automatically. We still don't know the reasons for the displayed results, and they may not know the context of our exploration, but it's very helpful nevertheless because it shows relevance.
- Product specialists or trained salespersons like the ones in Best Buy, or online chat sessions with agents, are another avenue for customers to turn to before they look somewhere else for reinforcement and answers on fitment. These conversations are very fruitful when they turn to "why are you buying this?" and "what else do you have?" Are the sources of information prepared

to effectively answer these questions? Are the customers being oriented to these sources so they come back for reinforcement throughout their decision cycle?

- Product selectors such as those on websites of credit card companies and car buying sites are yet another step forward towards helping customers validate their selection. They help put the customer's need in perspective. But these serve information from their perspective, not from the customers'. I would think that Amazon would have dozens of product selectors in its arsenal by now. But I guess it's complicated to compare and recommend from thousands of similar products. In my personal view, most customers will visit Amazon.com after they have researched a product to close the transaction. However in a more competitive online retail scenario where advantages of pricing are disappearing, context setting may actually be very useful in countering external reinforcement.

To illustrate the gap in the customer journey, think of customer reviews available on affiliate websites and the many independent review forums. These are important tools for customers when a product meets their base level criteria (price, features, brand etc.) and they often proceed to validate their choices and preferences there. How they treat our products and position them to customers is obviously beyond our control.

Simply put, external reinforcement is validation of fit, choice, applicability and value. Everything in the world has an alternative. No product is indispensable. If you talk to people, you'll be surprised to know the many different reasons – sometimes completely bizarre to you – as to why they use the products or services they do. That's one of the reasons we have so many types of products meeting the same needs. Customers will typically buy after serious consideration of these factors, whether provided by you or by your competitors. The breadth and comprehensiveness of the customer's analysis will depend on multiple factors such as availability of information, fitment with needs, urgency of need, and affordability. Objectivity is expected in the external reinforcement process. Being on the right channels to provide customers this information in the manner they are likely to trust and absorb is a key challenge that is met through the Principle of External Reinforcement.

For this reason, mere technologies that enable uplifts of our traditional outbound promotions based cross-sell and offer based marketing practices will not suffice in the new digital world. It won't matter how automated the new tool is, firms investing in digital transformation programs with a traditional marketing model as the foundation will have to change again – dramatically. And perhaps even be caught in a fight for survival. Because while the tools enable them to fix a business process shortcoming with technology, they must also be building a vision for looking at the true customer experience, the way customers want it, and the way customers actually engage. Helping customers perform this analysis makes for a perfect partnership. As customers become more accustomed to our services, build their preferences and in general become more aware of the competitive landscape, the percentage of the "right customers" increases.

Acquiring the Right Customers in the Right Way

The acquisition of "right customers in the right way" is not a trivial matter, or one solely based on integrity and morality.

As an illustration of the right way, consider the issues of customer retention in banking for add-on products and services. Research has shown that one of the primary reasons for customer dissatisfaction arises from poorly explained or unexplained benefits and features. Even after tweaking retention rewards – incentives to stay - and improving customer service quality:

- The retention levels continue to suffer
- The costs of retention climb
- Brand and customer service perception are damaged

The real reason that often remains unaddressed is that customers – across all industry segments - frequently have inadequate information about why they really needed the service they are subscribed to. This results in a constant tug of war with their conscience. And the first available external reinforcement of the fear results in a call to action. In other words, their reasons for buying the service do not match up with the perceived value the product really offers. In addition, a large percentage of customers who buy the service as a bundled package believe that their needs are being partially met through other products. Customer retention becomes a challenge because the external reinforcement provided to the customers is either insufficient or inaccurate. Worse, since these products are generally 3rd party products with limited integration with the customer's own bank, there is insufficient reinforcement provided by the product itself. In reality, the services or products may offer better value as compared to alternative options. Every customer lost sooner than the time needed to recover the investments causes a big dent in profitability. This brings up an important dimension of the Principle of External Reinforcement which is often forgotten in light of misaligned incentives.

"It's not only preferable to partner with the customer and help them make the right choice, but it's mandatory to do so to preserve your own profitability and future viability."

Each adverse – or even neutral - customer experience triggers a chain of events that may not show impact in the short term, but will dent customer perception, product differentiation, and the organization's brand in the long term. In today's business environment, competitive advances secured through methods that are not a hundred percent aligned with customer partnership will yield the unintended and undesirable results below:

Table 1: Effects of lack of customer partnership

Effect	What it implies
Struggle to acquire and retain customers	• No clear way to differentiate • Constant price promotions • Higher sales costs
Long term failure in terms of reputation	• Falling out of favor • Confused target market • Low referral sales
Misaligned internal organizational culture	• Inability to innovate • Inability to build on strengths • Unable to keep up competitive parity

These dire consequences create a market scenario where a new entrant will positively and comprehensively steal the incumbent's market share. Recent advances in all industries are examples of this trend. In financial services we are witnessing "simple and direct" as a theme, where as in consumer products we are witnessing "transparency and ecofriendly" as the overarching trend.

Do customers trust us? Or do they consider us to be selling machines of which they should be wary?

Customer partnership forces us to innovate, and is thus a required aspect of marketing and strategy. Examples are all around us in the form of companies that failed to ride the latest wave of the digital revolution. There are many valid reasons, and I believe one of the significant contributing factors is that our inertia restrains us from moving beyond defending what we have and trying to prove it to the customer. Often, most business leaders are aware of and would like to begin from the perspective of customer experience, but organizational factors make it difficult. Otherwise, many of the brand names we loved in the past would still be around today.

Our journey as customers has important implications for who will succeed in winning our business, and that of our networks, now and also in the future. In fact, one of the first things we do when we look up a product online is to look at comparative ratings and product reviews by others. If we find helpful reviews, research tools, and satisfactory educational product information on the website we initially visit, and if the purchase timing is right, then we are likely to make a purchase right then, or at least come back to the same website and make our purchase – and perhaps many subsequent ones. Similar criteria exist for B2B sales as well although complexity and length of the sales cycles and mediums of information vary significantly.

We need to be hooked onto the source (or seller) as a "partner." It must become our anchor. Otherwise, we continue to research and look elsewhere for an anchor – online or physical. It's a perfectly natural and an expected course of action. How this customer experience unravels is the key to defining our chances of buying the service or product from a particular source. If the initial engagement lets us go without establishing a connection with us, then it gives up the control, and the need for external reinforcement prominently steps in. That's the very reason why marketing is different from sales. It must create a strong relationship with the customer in addition to raising awareness, running promotions and offering other incentives. When boundaries between marketing and sales are diffused, we lose control of the customer conversation. And we end up fighting a faceless, commoditized battle. Yes, the outcome of marketing may be to set up the sale, but that's not its purpose. It's a crucial difference in the digital world.

The Principle of External Reinforcement aims to satisfy our unexpressed motivations in addition to just selling and pitching.

1. We look for a validation of our decision. Should we even buy what we are looking for? Are there any other options that help us to meet the need?
2. Once our decision is validated, we look for a validation of the products we choose. Do they really meet what we are looking to do? How well do they do so?
3. Then we look for a validation of applicability and interoperability. "Does this television integrate well with the capabilities of my XBOX?" "How does this enterprise software integrate with my existing technology landscape?"
4. Finally, we examine in more detail the best supporting actors; price, shipping, installation, accessories etc.

All of these customer questions and needs are continuous and happen through the purchase lifecycle. We look for supporting actors even as we validate our decision and shortlist products. In addition, strong customer engagement in the post-purchase phase helps in making those positive experiences available to others making the same decisions.

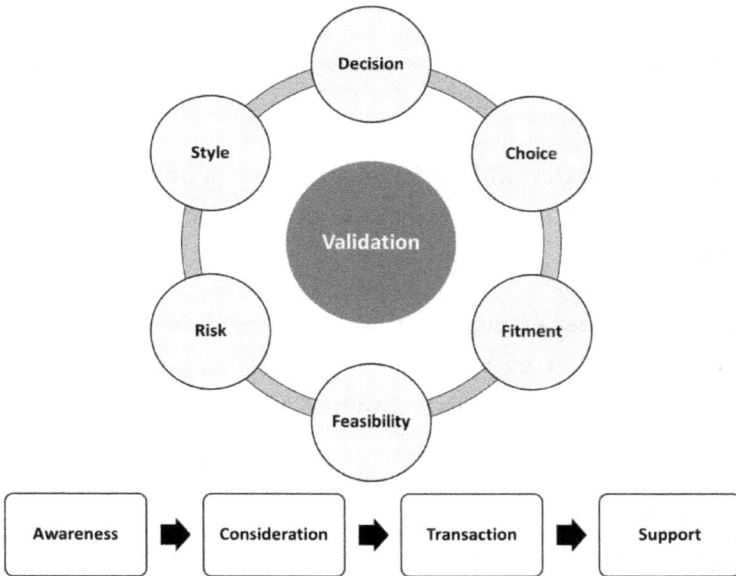

Figure 2: Validation of needs at various stages of the relationship

These validation questions also imply that traditional engagement approaches that focus on showcasing the product itself are inadequate. Sure, most sales today are provided through attractive offers and promotions, but it is still a numbers game. Relevancy and effectiveness - and hence total cost of sales – can be vastly improved by carefully addressing the needs for external reinforcement.

- Help customers make the right decision about their choices
- Help customers make a conscious choice about us
- Help customers feel good about their choices

- Help customers with changes in circumstances

When we base the customer relationship on value as measured by them, the customers are proud of their choice of product and about working with us. This automatically helps retention rates, decreases service costs, as well as increases the total lifetime value of the customer measured by repeat or cross-sell / up sell.

$$\textit{Lifetime value} \propto \textit{Retention rates} + \textit{Service costs} + \textit{Cross sell} + \textit{Up sell}$$

The Principle of External Reinforcement aims to address these needs for validation as it establishes a trusted-connection with the customer.

For strong customer engagement, we must validate and reinforce the customer's choice at every stage of the relationship by helping to assess changes in needs, product innovation or evolving circumstances.

1. Validation of Decision

A customer's purchase cycle starts long before they start looking at products. The first thing they establish is a desire or a need – either real or emotionally felt. The decision to explore options and do something about the perceived need is different from evaluating a product.

- Prestige: Wear an expensive watch
- Social: Have friends over and watch football games on a large screen TV
- Practical need: Buy a new car to drive to work
- Recognition: Be known as an expert in a field
- Management: Improve the work efficiency of our department

- Marketing: Enhance the website of our company to provide a different experience

And so on.

Just as there are different customer segments, there will be different types of needs that your business will want to fulfill. A need or desire often begins with an experience and a sentiment.

Not all needs will end up resulting in an action by customers to fulfill them. Some will be rejected, some will get postponed, some will be accepted with reservation, some will become experiments, and some will be accepted. Our affluence, culture, social influence, and inherent nature are all factors that play a role. The principle of external reinforcement strives to anticipate the customer's emotional and real sentiments to provide them with the right information about making the decision to move forward. The goal is not to sell, but to help the customer make a choice that is suited to his environment and his goals.

- "Do I really need something new to meet my need or can I meet it by other means?"
- "Should I buy what I am looking for?"

These decisions could be regarding simple impulse purchases. But customers do need to make them.

The Principle of External Reinforcement strives to become a partner to the customer as they contemplate this decision. In later sections, we will address why resisting the urge to sell, and helping customers in an unbiased manner with this question may seem counterintuitive, but is probably the best strategy in this digital and social world. This is becoming an accepted model for complex business-to-business sales models and in the new connected world is very relevant to the business-to-consumer models as well. Establishing a connection at this stage means that we have earned one of the top spots in the customer's mind. They will come back to us repeatedly as they sort this decision out, and the chances are high that they will ultimately buy from us.

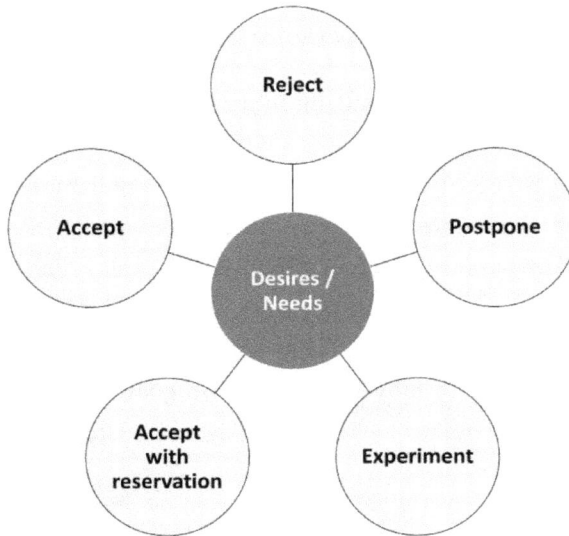

Figure 3: Typical responses to desires and needs

For businesses with repeat purchases – or those that need sustained customer engagement such as business accounts - the need for external reinforcement reduces as positive experiences with the products increase. But that model is of interacting with customers to build engagement, and is more appropriately tackled in the next chapter on The Principle of Customer Interaction.

2. Validation of Product Choice

Now that the customer has made a decision to proceed, which products should be on the customer's shortlist? What other products and brands could they be looking at? What defines them?

It has been drilled into sellers to "always close the deal." And that tendency has moved to the online world as well. But the very fact that we are creating a brand in these changing times needs a different approach. Just like we dislike hard-nosed salesmen, we are not fully satisfied with techniques that try to take advantage of our impulsive nature by making us decide in light of insufficient information. We'd like the digital world to be consultative. It wasn't the case when there was less content to consider, but it's changing every day. Listing many products is not helping. Nor is dumping data on the customers and expecting them to decide what is right for them.

What customers need is an educated push in the direction they should be taking. Customers look for external reinforcement, either in person, in their online social networks, online communities or through other sources. And once we lose control of the conversation in this manner, it's purely by chance that they come back to us. Sources of external reinforcement may or may not work out in our favor.

- I was willing to experiment with the many services that have come up recently that offer pre-packaged, pre-measured ingredients to make it easy to cook at home. Unsure about the process, I held out until a colleague who used such a service educated me about it. And she sent me a free offer from the service she used herself. It was different from the service that had engaged me before.

Just as we examined the model in the previous "Validation of Decision" step, we'll examine a similar model here as well. How should a product be pushed to customers after they have made a decision to purchase something? This is by no means easy for companies to achieve. The very notion of not pushing our product in the guise of help and advice is alien to many of us. It's a painful experience to just talk about the customers need but not actively position our products. But to ensure that the customer will have a great experience with your product, that is exactly what is needed.

- Which of our products best match customers' needs best?
- Which of our products do NOT meet customers' needs?

By engaging in such a dialog with the customers, we establish a reference benchmark in the customers' minds. The benchmark is used to compare and evaluate other products. And, customers will come back to the trusted benchmark for validation. In fact, the very reasons that cause our product to not be a fit for them at the present time may become important factors in the decision over time.

- An enterprise customer may not respond to claims about a better product that helps meet future needs. At the present time, price may be an important factor in the buyers mind. But if instead of pushing the product, we focus on helping to elaborate customer needs, it is likely that along the decision cycle, the scalability and future readiness factor will become as important as or even more important than price.

Such an approach helps to provide external reinforcement to the customer by becoming a part of the decision instead of being the subject of it. Discussions about total cost of ownership and workshops are an effective tool to achieve this objective. By meeting the external reinforcement requirements, we establish a reference benchmark in the customers' minds. To establish the reference benchmark, it is important to provide a balanced view. Selling in the guise of advising does not work.

It may seem that this model does not apply to commodity products. While the focus on short term sales should definitely be maintained, when that product is backed by a brand that the company is trying to build, the customer partnership approach is absolutely required. A product only becomes a commodity when companies make it a commodity. Let's put ourselves in the consumer's shoes. When we go to the store, do we look for both price and brand, or do we make a decision by price alone? Does a low price look better when we consider the brand as well? For me, both matter. But with every passing day that the brand doesn't connect with me or appeal to me with their promise, the brand continues to weaken. Why them? Taste tests, recipes, demonstration of quality, sources of ingredients, showing off the results, expert testimonials, child-friendliness etc. are all important methods in the real world to maintain emotional engagement.

Accepting that a commodity positioning is required to sell in a competitive world is by itself a death knell to the brand. It soon percolates all the way across the organization – from product development to marketing. Building a real position and a brand is a difficult endeavor. But customers do pay a premium for it. The premium is made up by both emotional and physical beliefs. Relegating the emotional connections to advertisements alone and fighting the real war on price affects how the product performs in the market. I'll address this in more detail in the next chapter on The Principle of Customer Interaction.

3. Validation of Fitment

Will this product work well with my other choices? And the products I already have? If I buy it, what could I do with what I already have? These are the lingering questions to which we always look for answers. That's why people want to talk to a real person in the case of complex products. And for a layman or novice user, there can be tremendous complexity in making the choice even for a simple product. That leads to hesitation, and that hesitation is a perfect opportunity for someone else to move in and claim the top spot in the customers' minds.

The Principle of External Reinforcement is a method to create a partnership with the customer so that this scenario is eliminated. Every interaction that a customer has with the product is an opportunity to not only meet their direct needs, but also to uncover opportunities within the immediate context and understand the overall ecosystem.

- Is a customer staring at yogurt in the grocery store contemplating a planned menu for an upcoming event? Or has she just started on a diet?
- Is a customer looking up retirement planning on a website looking to switch his portfolio, improve it or initiate it?
- Is a visitor coming to your website through a search on e-Commerce products looking to switch providers or products?

These are simplistic scenarios. The point is that designing processes around analysis of fitment will help you counter the forces of external reinforcement. What can we do on every channel that can cater to the needs of fitment? Either present products in context, or allow customers to explore products by selecting a context.

4. Validation of Feasibility

Feasibility is the supporting actor who makes it possible for the star to win the award. The trick is to ensure that the supporting actors don't overshadow the stars. Price, shipping, installation, accessories, after sales and service are supporting actors. They must be right to ensure that the experience carries all the way through, but they cannot carry the show on their own. These examples from sitcoms illustrate the point:

- George, Elaine and Kramer are the pillars that enable the full Seinfeld experience to come through. Without them, would the episodes have been as funny?
- Have you watched Frasier? Without Niles and Roz, where would Frasier have been?
- What about Friends? What makes the entire cast stick together and dazzle? Would any more focus on the stars have made it as effective?

Come to think of it, in any successful sitcom, the lead doesn't ultimately carry the show, it's the supporting cast. But without the lead, everything still feels empty. Contrast Seinfeld, Friends and Frasier with the work of the actors in subsequent shows. They weren't as successful because the entire focus was on the leads. They were expected to carry the show on their own.

In fact, we can argue forever about who are the main stars in each of the shows and we can produce brilliant arguments either way. That's exactly the point. The supporting cast gels so well with the main star that the strength is in the entire experience. Without one, the other feels empty. And it takes effort to strike the right balance.

In our case, the supporting actors are either easily commoditized (price, shipping) or take a long time to really build up (service, quality) because they need to be recognized, quoted and experienced. They must be part of the overall package instead of being expected to "win the war" on their own.

5. Validation of Risk

When we do something new, we take a risk - the risk of the unknown. How we mitigate the risks in a customer's mind drives how fast the customer makes a decision. The risk is not necessarily of the product, but more about:

- Returning to the physical status quo if the trial fails: It must be easy to recover our losses. For an ecommerce business, effortless and reliable return / exchange of goods and refund of payment are critical. How would we return the customer to status quo if we fail?
- Meeting intangibles: For a new dad-to-be buying a camera, the prospect of losing his memories far outweighs the few dollars saved. Similarly, for a busy sales person, spending the time to try out and return items may be a daunting activity.

What risks are we expecting our customers to take? How are we validating their risk? And how are we helping to resolve the issues if / when the risks come true?

6. Validation of Style

This is the 360 degree loop that matches the personality of a person to the product. This is the final building block and could very well have been the first one to start the journey. An emotional connection, an appeal to a person's inner desires may have started them on this journey to decide whether or not to buy. If not, then this aspect will definitely bring them closer to you in the final phases of their decision making.

For enterprise sales, this is the culture of the company, or the feeling of associating with experts. After the mechanics are done, you need that final emotional thread of support to complete your decision.

Without that, you don't feel secure.

For consumers, it's about connecting with their inner desires and dreams. Wouldn't you want to be like the athlete who's holding on with sheer grit even as his body is screaming for rest, the athlete who kicks the ball to score the winning goal in pouring rain or the rugged adventurer who makes her way up a winding road in the mountains to come across the most beautiful view on earth? Yes! That's the dream. We resolve to complete the challenge and win. That's who we want to be. We stand a little straighter. We want to commit to that goal. And it helps us move forward with confidence that we are doing the right thing.

Of course, there's a lot to be done about continuing the reinforcement post-purchase. Experiences after purchase feed external reinforcement and make it relevant and contextual.

External reinforcement can be triggered by any of the above sources. If the channel the customer is on doesn't do ANY of the validation, and if it just screams at them to buy the product and keeps telling them how great the product is, then the customer has to:

- Figure out the answers to all their questions
- Decode the product specifications to their need
- Understand what the reviews are really saying
- Research competitors
- Fit a product to his/her needs
- Find a match with the brand promise and style

In short, we are leaving all the work to the customer and hoping they miss some of the issues we have, and somehow make a decision in our favor because we have advertisements in all the right places. These types of wins are short lived.

It's easy to fall into the trap of looking at the short term, field level tactics and wonder why we cannot continue to pursue the same. After all, they are delivering results and we are winning, right? In the new digital world, the Principle of External Reinforcement takes the long term view. It implies building a trusted position in the customer's mind. Because if we don't counter the effects of external reinforcement and fail to set ourselves up as a partner to the customer, the result will be equivalent to death by a thousand cuts. That's because while we are getting accustomed to acquiring and maintaining customers that way, someone else is building the foundation for the future.

Worse, by not being pushed everyday by the drive to partner with the customer, our organizational culture will evolve and adapt to the tactical, short term results orientation. And we won't be able to transform it when we really, really need to. The culture of an organization is a complex behavior. We can't put a finger on it, but we know we're up against it when we need it the most. That's the dramatic long term impact.

The Non-Linearity of External Reinforcement

Understanding what a customer needs to become interested, perform research and make a decision has always been important for strategists. But the real difference in execution comes from how we act and built upon that information about our customers in this new age.

Let's think about it for a minute. How customers seek external reinforcement is not a linear path. Although we are all aware of the journey from awareness to purchase, the actual behavior is pretty complex. We've simplified the journey, because it makes it easier to comprehend the specific challenges at each stage, take appropriate actions and devise measurement criteria.

How should we address the need for external reinforcement when we are striving to build loyalty and brand recognition in a competitive marketplace? How do we address fear and ignorance?

- If we tell our customers why our product category (or our product itself) may be bad for them (or not right for them), won't our sales suffer?
- If we mention our competition on our website, are we not providing free advertising for them?
- Even if I were to do the above, how would I make sure I'm covering all the bases so it won't backfire?
- How would I explain this to my boss and peers, who are steeped in traditional marketing?
- There are likely to be setbacks and/or slow progress. How would I know what's normal?

These questions cannot be taken lightly, because there is significant potential for adverse impact. In addition, we cannot make changes that are just window dressing. Instead, our analysis of the situation and the actions we take should be geared towards this one question: What should we be doing so we can prove to the customer that we are their best choice?

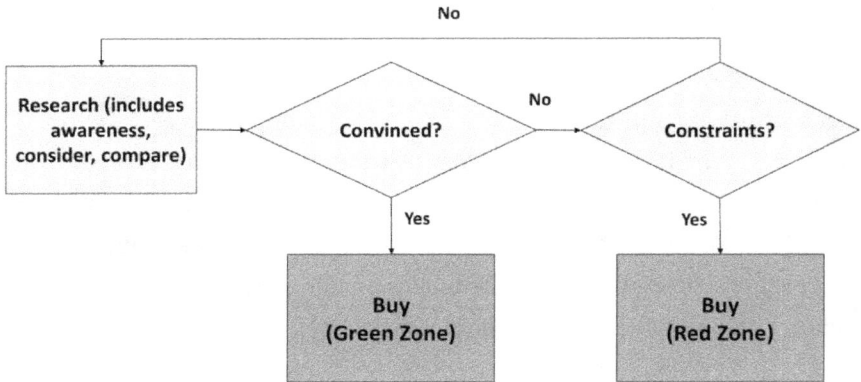

Figure 4: Being in the green zone is important for total lifetime value

In our day and age of information abundance, and often misinformation abundance, hiding or not acknowledging facts, and perceptions lead to the increased need for external reinforcement. The only effect of not providing information is that customers look to sources other than ours to validate if we may be a good fit. And those sources may not do justice to our case. In fact, these sources may even sell the customer a worse product or our most intense competitor.

As shown in the figure above, relying on customer constraints to make a sale is not a great idea as it may lead to continuous re-evaluation of choice, which may be detrimental for referral sales, not to mention low repeat sales, high cost of retention, and increased post sales service costs if applicable.

For products that are inherently similar or even the same (commodities), and those that rely more on branding, non-product attributes (supporting actors) and emotional connections with users, it is even more important to supplement the brand promise by providing external reinforcement. The consumer not only experiences our brand frequently but is under constant siege by the industry through promotions, trials, advertising and other marketing tools. It's important to continue to raise the barriers rather than rely on price discounts. If we don't reinforce, consumers will be forced to look elsewhere, and we will lose control of the conversation.

The stand we take is the all-important question, the answer to which will galvanize the brand. We will automatically come to answer all important questions based on:

1. The focus of our brand
2. The way we market
3. Our organization's culture

Figure 5 outlines the non-linear aspect of the customer journey. The phases I have labeled as "reinforcement zones" show how customers will always need to be supported in their decision making – whether it is before purchase, during or after purchase. Reinforcement zone 3 includes post-purchase reinforcement that builds confidence in the customer's choice and helps them feel good about the results they are getting (or working towards expected results). Instead of starting from the beginning, reinforcement zone 3 compliments zones 1 and 2. For business-business models, zone 3 is an important vehicle for cross-sell and also for referral sales.

The needs are different at different stages, and the reinforcement must be designed accordingly to minimize the need to go to external sources. In summary, that means that our reinforcement must be from a customer's perspective, not ours.

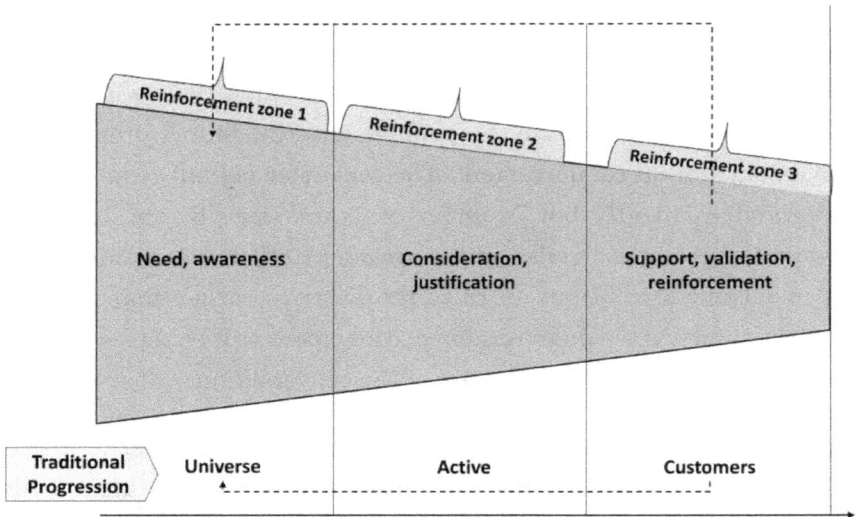

Figure 5: Reinforcement zones of the non-linear customer journey

Zone 1 has received a lot of attention. The real impact will be through zone 2 and zone 3, and how all three are unified. With advances in technology such as marketing automation, physical barriers to entry into a reinforcement program have become much less. However the biggest barriers continue to largely remain in place and have to do with:

1. Understanding what our customers want to achieve
2. Helping them achieve their goals
3. Meeting the metrics of our business

The Different Patterns of Reinforcement of Choices

The Principle of External Reinforcement does not follow a universal pattern because it depends on how the customer interacts with our product at every stage of their journey. It varies for different types of products, companies and customers. Some products may call for much more social engagement than others because they are either frequently purchased or are conducive to a community effect that helps build an emotional connection with customers. Some may require only providing best practices and competitive information to sophisticated buyers, while some may only need alliances with partners that actually interact with the customer. Looking at our product, our customer segment and how customers interact with our own and other sources to gather information in order to make a decision is important for meeting their needs of external reinforcement.

In other words, the strategies to meet The Principle of External Reinforcement require an understanding and outlining of the customer journey. Identifying the right pattern for our organization is an important step towards defining the business processes that we will adopt. The position we assume has to be supported across multiple channels and mediums to provide the same customer experience, education and information required to make us the trusted advisor, and their first port of call when the need arises.

As customers search for information today, they do so across multiple mediums and channels. It's not deliberate, it's just natural. How do we prioritize which channels and mediums to focus on? Our analysis of the customer journey leads to the answer. The assessment of channels is akin to the principle of uplift in market mix analysis – how do we spend our money on the set of customers (in our case this is channels and mediums) who have the highest probability of conversion, instead of spreading ourselves too thin? This analysis has far reaching impact on operational costs, organizational culture and customer experience.

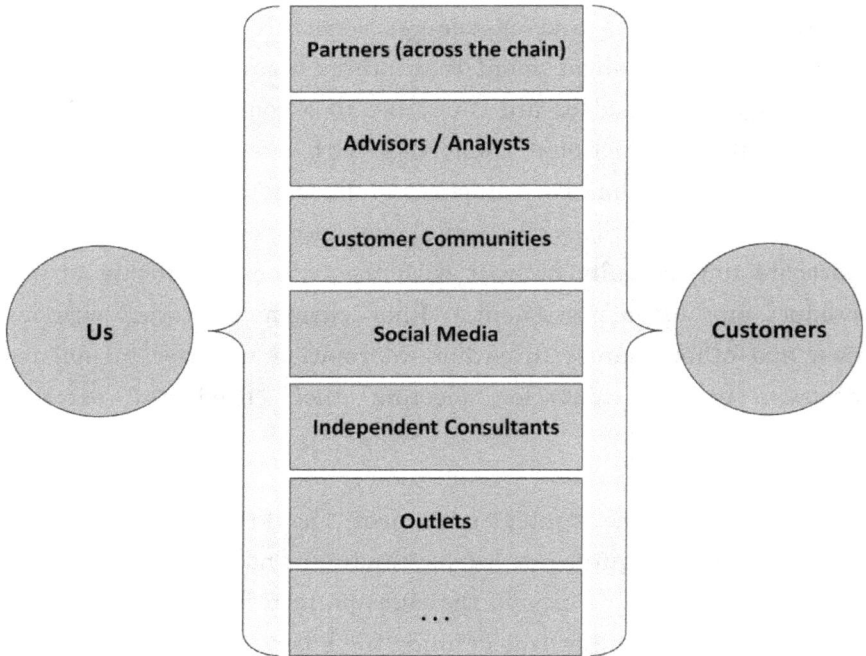

Figure 6: External reinforcement needs a clear assessment of channels

- Customers looking for a new car will search aggregator sites, call dealers, visit the dealers' websites among other things all the while looking for reviews, price differences, ease of buying, and evaluating if the car is right for them. If we were in the car business, would we not want to ensure that the customer is guided in the right manner? In order to do that, we would consider our ecosystem to include those channels of information, and allow them to channel the right customers to us.

- Similarly, an enterprise technology buyer will look to independent sources such as analysts, advisors, partners and other customers to make the best choices. They may hire consultants to help them map their needs to the services and products of their potential vendors.

The Principle of External Reinforcement is about being where our customers are and providing them with solid, reliable and neutral information. We may consider ourselves as both a generator and curator of information available about our products and services, as well as a source of honest advice about what's right for the customer. As we have seen, selfishness only helps in the short term and has disastrous consequences on the organizational culture over the long term. If we are looking at all the brand activity on social media today, everybody is talking, but very few are counseling or listening. It's easy to talk, but it's very difficult to counsel especially when it means our product may not be the best fit in a specific scenario. This relates to one of the universal laws of branding which is to define ourselves clearly and take a stand. To attract the best customers and others along with them, we have to go beyond speaking, and look to be a partner in their choice.

External reinforcement goes beyond selling our products and services, and prioritizes meeting customer needs, both tangible and intangible. And that implies we must know where we want to go as a company and what stand we're going to take. We'll address this in more detail in Chapter 3 on The Principle of Un-Commoditization. This thinking percolates throughout our organization, shows in every interaction we make with our market and ultimately makes us passionate and more appealing to our customers. The purpose of an organization is to meet needs, and that action translates to revenues, happy people and shareholder value. Reversing the purpose is easy but the consequences are not pretty.

Understanding how to reinforce the customer is a prerequisite to properly defining how and where we wish to communicate. It's easy to develop strategies based on the outcome of analytics. However, most businesses do not have, or haven't compiled the right "subjective" data on their customers. The basic questions of who, where, why are important to answer to channel our efforts in the right direction. But these alone won't be enough to satisfy the Principle of External Reinforcement. What we really need to do is develop how we will satisfy the need for external reinforcement. How we will answer the questions being asked, when we will stand up and say we're NOT the right choice, and how we will get embedded into the networks of our customers. For example, for complex engineering products, neutral expert advice is often sought to decide between products. It's important to understand these additional sources as we understand our customer's journey so we can address these channels.

Product selection is always on merit, and merit is not decided by quality alone. Merit is determined by what customer needs and motivations are. In some cases, they are about price, in some cases they are longevity, and in other cases they are about ease of working together, culture, reputation, style and so on. In fact, the factors that define merit could be anything - place of manufacture, color, culture of company, service, friendliness etc. That's why customer research and segmentation is important. It is of paramount importance to analyze and understand. We cannot be everything to everyone. This adopting The Principle of External Reinforcement also supplements branding and product strategies.

Removing Barriers to External Reinforcement

It is true that the urge to provide feedback and engage on the brand is stronger when we've had either a strongly negative or positive experience. In other cases, most consumers or customers don't bother to engage, or don't know how to engage. And the key reasons always come down to the barriers to external reinforcement.

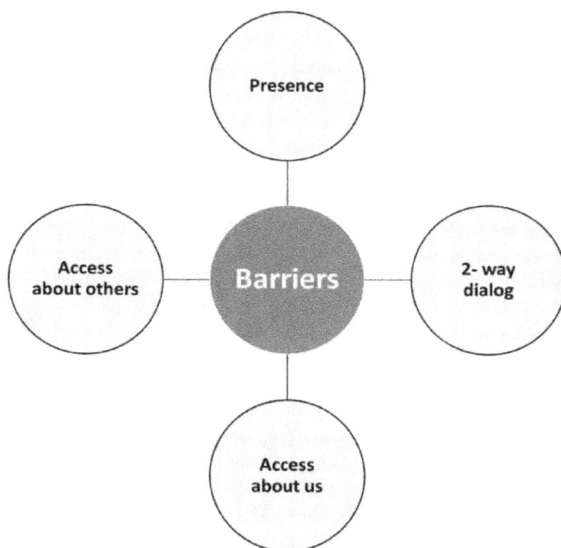

Figure 7: Tactical barriers to external reinforcement

1. Our presence on the right forums

The simplest barrier is our presence on the channels that customers frequent. Are we aware of, and present on the common physical and electronic channels? Are we missing discussions blogs, physical stores, forums, review sites etc.?

2. Opening a two-way communication channel

Mere presence is the first step. Are customers able to communicate with us in a simple manner or do they have to jump through hoops to speak with us? The investments we make and the returns we expect will be determined by the frequency and target market alignment of the channel, but it must be on our radar, nevertheless.

3. Good access to what others are saying about us

Customers know what they have to say, and they also know what we have to say. External reinforcement implies that they must be able to reflect upon their experiences in light of what others have to say. This ecosystem can be a powerful rationalizer of negative emotions, and a strong amplifier of positive emotions.

4. Good access to what others are saying about others

If the channels are all about us, then that's only half the battle won. The popularity of comparison or review sites stems from the fact that many parties get to talk and participate. We need to promote a stand on the product category and the need it tries to solve. By doing that, and by talking less, we take home more fodder for our innovation pipeline, and nurture the customer to decide in our favor.

Meeting the needs for external reinforcement is a positioning, customer research and customer partnership approach that needs to be well planned and executed. Next, let's look at how such a plan can be developed.

Developing a plan for meeting the needs of external reinforcement

So far we've looked at the following requirements for external reinforcement:

1. Adapting to the path taken for decision making
2. Understanding the patterns of information sharing and acquisition

It's time to shift gears and outline the two maturity levels of customer partnership through the Principle of External Reinforcement.

Educating & Advising

Selling

Figure 8: The two maturity levels of customer partnership

At the first maturity level, we are selling:

1. Why us?
2. Benefits to you
3. Our pricing
4. Our references
5. Our awards
6. Our clients
7. Our size
8. Our etc.

At this maturity level, it's all about us and our product, and how it meets the needs of the customer. We are trying to sell who we are, and our value proposition.

But the customer is pushing us and our isolated approach away. We are isolated because we ignore our competitors and the overall needs of our customers in the dialog with our customers. The competition and other market forces are behind why we exist, but it's hidden from the customer. We rely on customers to make the choice in our favor. And to do that we provide them the tools they need to make that decision about their problem. The selling approach is isolated because we are all about us. We don't elaborate on the fitment of our solution with their overall needs spectrum, and we definitely don't advertise why our product or service may not be right for the customer. These choices are implicit in our strategy, segmentation and our marketing and selling efforts, but not when we go to market.

In short, we fight against the principle of external reinforcement instead of using it to our advantage to build customer partnerships. We push and we prod, we become visible, and we try to inject ourselves in every customer interaction and inquiry. We try to speak louder and clearer and advertise how we are the ideal choice.

And yet, the real moment of truth comes when we stop fighting, and instead align with and leverage the principle of external reinforcement.

We then move to the second level of maturity when we begin to think of the customer:

- Are these products even relevant to you?
- What you should be looking at before you make a decision?
- Where do we fail to meet your needs? Is that a good tradeoff?
- Which features are most relevant for you?

- What long term trends in this area are relevant for you?
- What preparation is important to future proof your business?
- Why you should NOT consider us?
- On what fronts is a competitor a better fit for you?
- How can we help minimize your risks in choosing us?
- Does having multiple products from us help you more?
- Does buying from multiple suppliers help you more?
- How will we address the challenges inherent in transitioning to us?

The difference is obvious. In both business-business and business-consumer scenarios, the very questions that marketers ask when evolving their products or defining their future strategy are important to position, market and sell, too.

It's a nerve wracking experience. How can we tell our customers we are not right for them? Especially when we advertise and market that we are the magic elixir. How can we not sell something in which we are investing?

And so we decide to just do our part and let the customer decide. And hope that they'll decide in our favor. As a result we give up control. And The Principle of External Reinforcement kicks in. By shifting the responsibility to the customer we open the doors wider for external reinforcement, and relinquish the grip on what should have been a joint decision.

It's best to think of the second maturity level as a double-effect strategy:

1. The short term effects

When we provide customers with answers they do not expect from us, we show both our strengths and vulnerabilities. It's not a traditional experience but it leads to an important result. Our customers begin to expect the same of our competition. And that's where the effects of aligning with the principle really begin to impact the short term. It begins to build trust. We become the benchmark and advisor, not just someone pitching their wares. The probability of winning may actually increase because we've caused the customer to think about their needs in a better way. If we are not chosen, we didn't lose anything. We would probably have lost anyway because the customer was not right for us. That's the new economy - where we cannot win for long by not opening ourselves up and working hand-in-hand with the customer, and the multiple channels with which they interact.

- Business-business: Are we stuck with low prices and low margins after on-boarding a customer in the wrong frame of mind? (E.g. accounts where prices are low, or which don't match the core-competencies of our organization). Are we struggling to prove our mettle and merit because our channel partners have aligned with others?
- Business-consumer: Do consumers speak highly of our product and the experiences after they've bought from us? Are the benefits of our channel partners fully aligned with our business scorecard? (E.g. travel packages, online retail or fashion products). Are there passionate communities that advocate our products over others?
- Business-consumer: Are we facing a high churn scenario where high acquisition rates are not yielding the expected ROI? (E.g. credit cards, consumer electronics and insurance products). Are we being relegated to being a provider of services, and giving up the customer interface to others?

Many of the examples above will also yield significant long term benefits by way of better reputation and credibility.

2. The long term effects

This is where the real prize is.

First, when we win, we win for the long haul, and start from a position of supreme strength and customer confidence. Our customers (and that includes channel and other partners) are not constantly going to be living with nagging fears about their choice. We don't have to constantly protect ourselves from mundane competitive offers to supersede us. Sure, retention strategies will still be needed, but from a position of strength.

Second, as we do this more often, our brand begins to gain strength. We become the customers' advocate, and they begin to speak to us first about what they should do, or how they should evaluate products.

Third, we perpetuate a culture of innovation and customer partnership throughout the organization. No longer are we trying to compete as a me-too, but the positive cycle of customer partnership kicks in. We are now looking to create value, and leapfrogging the current demands. Our eye is on the market, on the trends, and how to use them to take the next step. We safeguard ourselves against disruptive innovation because we are becoming the disruptive force.

Fourth, positive traction helps keep up and drive the momentum. Every organization needs a vision and a drive to be motivated to the cause. We dig, we improve and we dig again. No one feels tired when they are on a mission. It's a challenge that keeps everyone alive.

In short, good things happen when we think of customer partnership. It may sound like customer partnership is about complex business-to-business models, but look around us. The best performing consumer brands are doing the same thing. The mechanics will be different, but the concept is the same.

How exactly do we meet the needs of the second maturity level?

1. By outlining and addressing the scenarios under which our customer segments may NOT need our products (adverse fitment).
2. By addressing the selection/comparison information and outlining our fit (fitment).
3. By providing education to this segment on making the most out of the product (advice, best practices and dos and don'ts)
4. By closing the gap between this target customer and what the current users in this segment are saying and recommending (evolution).

Summary – The Principle of External Reinforcement

The principle of external reinforcement is about creating an ecosystem where the need for a customer to look for external sources is minimized. In other words, to operate at the second level of maturity, we sell to them by not selling - help them make the right choice instead of just asking them to choose us. And the more comprehensive and honest we make our presence across the channels and sources of information, the more game changing our position becomes.

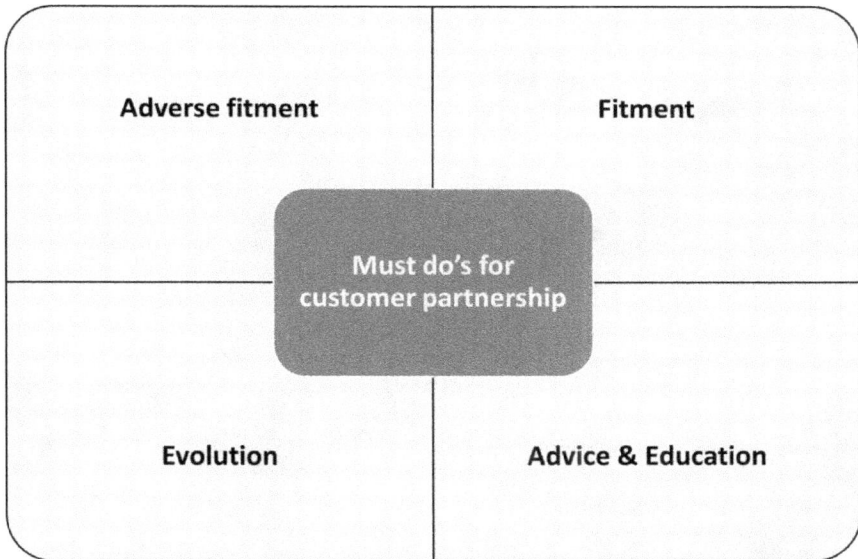

Figure 9: Parameters for meeting the second maturity level of customer partnership

2

The Principle of Customer Interaction

The Principle of Customer Interaction brings together the emotional and fulfillment (physical) ends of the customer interaction spectrum. Interaction patterns are different for different types of products. We must develop our ability to engage and interact so that both ends of the customer interaction spectrum are active and aligned with each other.

Have you sometimes felt emotionally disconnected with the brands you use? Do you feel you are not really experiencing the brand's promise? Do people around you speak of product features and aspects that you aren't aware of or haven't really used?

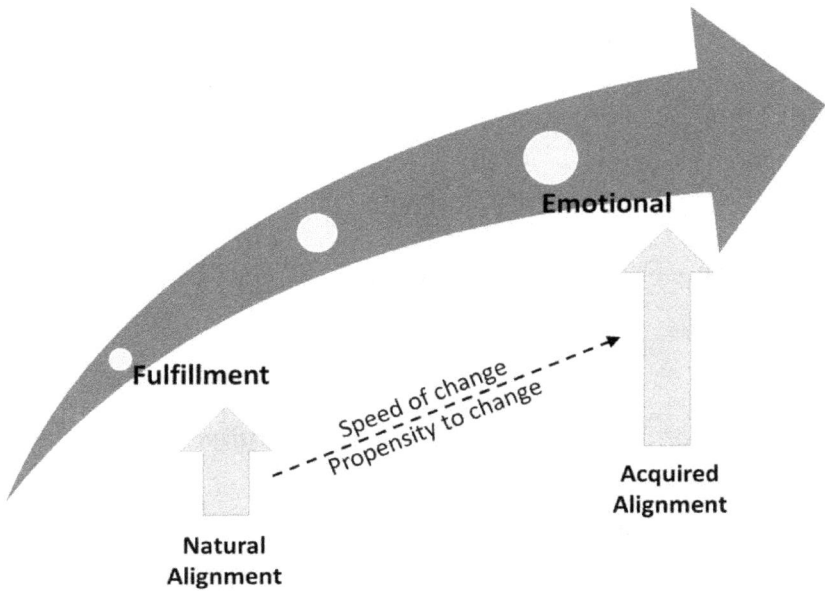

Figure 10: The Customer interaction spectrum

The Principle of Customer Interaction is about understanding and aligning the two ends of the interaction spectrum – emotional and physical. It is not about gimmicks to attract people and get them to buy. Instead, it enables us to decipher customer interaction patterns that our products and industry lend themselves to. And in turn, that helps us take appropriate measures to engage customers in a much more conscious and strategic manner. The more our customers "use and experience" our products, in a way that's aligned with the brand promises we are projecting, the more likely they are to be engaged consciously. In case our customers really shouldn't be using our products frequently (like perhaps a fire extinguisher), or they are not customers yet, then experiencing our products promise by way of other immersion techniques such as education, demonstrations, training and best practices information will boost customer engagement.

In short, The Principle of Customer Interaction is about ensuring that the physical and emotional spectrums of customer experience are in sync with each other. The customer engagement metric, if sensibly used, is a good proxy for higher acquisition, retention and cross-sell and up-sell metrics. It often leads to and influences these metrics in a very clear way.

- Why does our favorite yogurt brand send us recipes for a cool summer salad? After all, we can use any yogurt brand in the recipe.
- Why do credit card companies offer us exceptional cash-back and other promotions to get us to activate our cards? Are they banking only on the likelihood that we won't stop once we start?
- Why do we get those free invitations to self-help seminars (business or personal)? Is the likelihood high of us finding something relevant in the content now or in the future (other than the chance to hard-sell a membership or a donation of course)?
- Why do we get to taste delicious samples at most food stores? That's a product promotion, but the store is probably doing better, too.
- Are we part of an online community that is backed by a corporation? (E.g. The Home Depot community). If we see a project there, are we more likely to head over to The Home Depot to initiate it?

These are the simplest of examples. But they clearly outline that engaging customers on both physical and emotional fronts is vital for business. And the digital economy makes it mandatory. If we don't engage customers this way, someone else will.

Understanding Customer Interaction Patterns

We already know that customers don't always interact with us in a set way.

- How they interact with a grocery store is very different from the way they interact with the company who makes their favorite toothbrush, or their car.
- Business customers interact in a different manner from how they interact with the manufacturer of the products they personally use.
- Within an industry, different customer segments and of course individual customers themselves behave and interact differently.

Due to the varied ways in which customers interact, understanding customer interaction patterns is the first step to defining models that boost customer engagement and loyalty.

The foundation of The Principle of Customer Interaction is that certain products or companies may have an inherent advantage in striking up a working and trusted relationship with the customers. These are firms that we interact with much more frequently and intimately. We don't leave them easily. We are even reminded of them several times a day even though we may not think twice about them. In other words these are transaction heavy companies that also have a face and a switching cost. Banks, credit cards, social networks, Google, cellphones, our grocery stores, a B2B supplier - you get the idea.

Then there are firms we interact with every day and who are linked to us in a slightly more emotional way- our clothes, shoes, perfume, the brand of chips, our favorite restaurant, our soap. We connect with the brands we use, we trust them and we talk about them, but the switching costs are low. We are open to experimentation. We are also highly prone to promotions based on price. We dream, we aspire, we identify, we belong and hence we are connected. The utility of the product itself is shaped by what we are made to believe, what it signifies, how it makes us feel and how it allows us to project ourselves. The product function is a criterion whose minimum performance threshold must be met in order for the brand to occupy this space in our minds. Product function is not even a consideration unless there is an anomaly that calls attention to it. It takes a physical or emotional shock to shake our habits when we are emotionally attached.

The Principle of Customer Interaction operates at both ends of the customer interaction spectrum:

1. Physical or natural alignment – arising from use and conscious interaction
2. Emotional or acquired alignment – arising from a perceived and emotional belief which may or may not be reinforced physically

The Principle of Customer Interaction implies that the ability to engage and interact is inherently much stronger when the fulfillment (or physical) and emotional ends of the interaction spectrum are connected. They both create avenues for customer engagement that complement each other. If the emotional level is not supported clearly by the physical, then the value of the brand is no longer clear. In such a case we still hold on to fantastic images of brand in our mind but given the lack of reinforcement, the end result is only generic differentiation - better, sophisticated, reputed. And the generic differentiation leads to a dilution of the power of the brand – easily exchangeable with other products that convey the same generic attributes, or those that send a powerful, differentiated message appealing to our senses.

Firms that have a high Customer Interaction Index generally have more frequent and more tangible interactions with their customers. For these firms, the customer engagement strategy must look at cementing engagement at the level of fulfillment and then constantly building on it to engage better at the emotional level, continuously changing, tailoring or improving the way they interact with the customer at the physical end of the spectrum. By the very nature of this industry, they have numerous occasions to interact directly with the individual customer. The customer is making a conscious choice to use their product and they both know about it.

Every such physical interaction should look to advance along the curve to the emotional end of the spectrum. In fact, every time we fail to do so due to lack of technical know-how, or other reasons that make it difficult to do so, it has two significant effects:

1. The lack of engagement raises the needed innovation threshold. That means more must be done to create stickiness and maintain parity with advances by our competition. Engagement at both ends of the spectrum creates a competitive barrier.
2. The lack of engagement also pushes us down the commoditization spiral. We must then use other mechanisms like price promotions and other incentives to acquire, or even hang on to, our customers.

Indeed brands are finding new ways every day to engage customers at both ends of the spectrum.

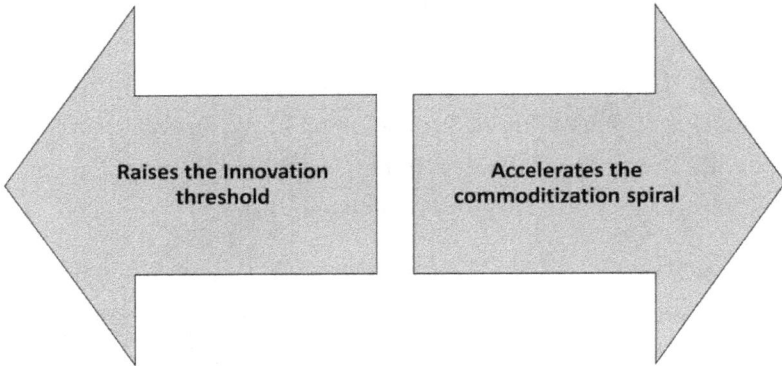

Figure 11: The effects of lack of engagement

- When we book a hotel room – or a travel package - through a travel site, we are encouraged to share our experiences, provide feedback or even connect with the persons who will be interacting with us. The more we do so, the more we are engaged at both emotional and physical ends of the spectrum.
- Every time we enjoy the gesture-based games on XBOX, the system takes amazing pictures that show happiness, fun and togetherness. Exceptional customer engagement opportunities through sharing experiences are being provided.
- Some very prominent manifestations are the Apple iTunes, Google Play and the Amazon Prime ecosystems. Such an ecosystem creates stronger and multi-faceted links with customers.

However, there is a lot more that can be done at both ends of the engagement spectrum in all of the cases above. We need only look at the entire lifecycle of the customer and compare it to the engagement avenues we are tapping into presently. Customer experience manifests in many ways. All of them arise from linking back physical or fulfillment experiences with the emotional positioning in the customer's mind.

- Every time we use our credit cards, we are providing the bank with valuable information in addition to everything the bank already knows about us. They know a great deal about us but are rapidly conceding the race for customer engagement to other players who actually provide the customer facing services. In my view, being content with being a back end provider of services is a dangerous proposition.
- Digital (and digital SLR) cameras have only recently begun to provide the ability for customers to share their memories. I wonder if that delay has caused the connected cameras in the iPhone and others to secure a comfortable place in the photography ecosystem. Decent quality, apps like Instragram and seamless connectivity with social networks has also promoted the use of these "alternative" cameras and brought them mainstream.

Digital cameras and banking are sound examples of why established businesses fail to rapidly keep pace with customer engagement. We are so product and business model focused that it's easy to lose touch with changing and evolving customer experiences. Even though the innovation is rapid, the impact is felt slowly and we stick to our "features" and tradition as a way to feel good about what we have always used. Surely, such sentiments must be controlled. Because they significantly start slowing down the way our business evolves to meet the impending wave of industry disruption. This trend first manifests itself in shifting customer retention trends to win customers back. Why wait for that moment even though we realize that the ground has shifted? Why not shift investment dollars early to correctly manage customer interaction?

On the other hand, as stories of the most famous brands indicate, the situation is reversed when the Customer Interaction potential is weak at the fulfillment level, but is driven from the emotional end of the spectrum. The engagement must be created at the emotional level (prestige, trust) which then automatically carries itself to the fulfillment level as the emotional needs are realized. This mass engagement model for these industries is in stark contrast to the individual model of engagement. That's what a large part of branding is all about - creating an emotional connection with the consumers and securing a position in the mind. Positions that define our brand, and help our customers choose, promote and defend the brand. In fact, once created the positioning is almost hard to dislodge, except with the passage of an appropriate length of time.

- As one of arguably most famous historical examples indicates, Coke has been winning in the market place even as taste tests often see Pepsi to be the preferred choice.
- We debate heatedly about adidas vs. Nike. Fans can probably put a finger on the differences between the actual products. In my view, constant discounts and promotions are diluting the specifics now.
- Ask a Honda fan about Harley Davidson, and they will wax eloquent about Honda's superior engineering quality. Then ask the same of a Harley Owner.
- The BMW is known as the Ultimate Driving Machine, and with so many models being launched, we can hear fans all over the world engaged in passionate debate on the definition of a driving

machine –luxury or performance?

That said, the importance of connecting at the fulfillment or physical level cannot be over emphasized for brands that have traditionally relied on the emotional end of the spectrum. When we consider the discount based promotional strategies, we have to wonder if the effects of the strong emotional branding are truly being leveraged to create long term differentiation. Are we forever going to be waging price wars to get and keep consumers? It's no doubt a complex strategic subject – one that includes the elements of the brand, customer segments, market share and growth. However, could perhaps billions of dollars be saved if brands can match their emotional connection to a physical connection with the customers at the fulfillment level of the spectrum?

- I love my significantly above average priced tennis racquet and my shiny branded sports apparel. But I am still losing matches everyday even after adorning myself with stuff that screams Wimbledon. In addition, I just advised a tennis newbie to just buy the cheapest racquet he can buy and focus on getting the shots right first. Is there an ecosystem that is wanting here?
- A colleague recently bought an expensive luxury car. There is no doubt that it's a great car, superior to the other more conventional cars. But how could his ideal customer experience be crafted so he can be reminded every day of his excellent choice? We asked him if his car can fly and drive on water. Of course it cannot. But other than talking about his brand perception, and showing us features that other cars in the same range also had, he wasn't really sure how to show off.
- When I fired up my pretty expensive television, I was left fiddling with the settings and exploring the show-off tricks on my own to achieve the mind-blowing experience I expected.
- When enterprises buy that expensive software product that

promises to make marketing contextual and relevant for their buyers, do they accomplish that painlessly or do they pour millions of dollars and still flounder with proving the business case?

We buy a brand, so why should our experiences be generic? Could we think about post purchase needs at the fulfillment level and cement the relationships further? How to show off, how to use, how to display the differentiation that really already exists – this is the essence of extending the brand promise across the customer interaction spectrum. Especially in today's connected world.

The Principal of Customer Interaction is about considering the physical and emotional connections customers make with our products, and ensuring that they complement each other. An absolute requirement of today's world is that physical experiences must complement the emotional connections we've established, and vice versa.

Without the emotional and physical ends of the spectrum in sync with each other, we end up fighting the discount war. All our outreach has to end in how the price is now attractive for our customers to buy from us. We are forever fighting the fear of our customers deserting us. And the funny thing is that what probably started as efforts to increase the brand loyal population is now a zero sum game.

It may seem that the issue of emotional and physical disconnect is true of smaller frequent purchases. But it's really not. Whether we buy an expensive television, enterprise software or an expensive car, we are looking for validation. Most likely the validation is there. We just have to find it. For such products, it's not about an impressive price to feature mapping because that's a given. The focus should be to ensure that our physical experiences match the capabilities of what that product promises to deliver. The physical experience of such products is probably inherently superior enough to match the emotional connection, and the delivery of the experience must match up, too.

Whether we are new to a product or very familiar, we need brands to look beyond the emotional connections they have with us - we may act like the sophisticated, all knowing, well-researched buyers, but that's just a façade. No one can hear it but we are calling desperately for help. We are begging for product and solution partners to validate our choices. Comfort with the familiar and fear of the unknown are barriers that are just waiting to be broken down by companies who can provide that additional interaction to make the transition easy. Customer experience is filled with holes today and we must recognize and bridge those gaps. Innovations in all industries are a testament to that - travel, hotels, payments, insurance, retail, logistics and the list goes on of traditional business models that are under threat due to the holes they failed to fill. As customers, we need to be aided by brands in becoming astute users. They must help us experience new ways of doing what we've always done. Otherwise, we'll do it on our own and the brands that think we love them will be left behind.

The Path to the Right Customer Experience

The emotional connect we establish becomes a combination of not only what has been advertised or promised, but also what has built up inside our heads because of what our imagination – supported by all the advertising - can dream up. We need to be gently and tactfully nurtured. Crafting the physical experience is a delicate combination of exciting customers, helping them accomplish their goals and at the same time making them aware that we are still on Earth. It's true of all products.

What can help craft the right customer experience? There are two basic rules:

1.   Defining the critical path to a compelling, WOW factor.
2.   Making it mandatory, not optional, to follow this critical path.

Most product innovations have a real and compelling story. Too often, in an effort to balance the tradeoff with customer flexibility, we dilute our value proposition. The question then also becomes of fit. If customers are not a fit for our products they won't enjoy them. They'll be the brand ambassadors who never were, perhaps even detractors who raise doubts in others' minds. As we saw when we discussed The Principle of External Reinforcement, the art of informed acquisitions is critical to identify and discourage impulse purchases that can be detrimental to our brand promise in the long run. For someone on a journey towards creating a lasting brand that doesn't rely on year round price discounts to sell, this is imperative.

When a sale is made, the cause for celebration is when the right sale has been made. And once again, that's true of a 60 cent can of soup or a home theater system worth several thousand dollars.

We've relied on mass marketing and branding techniques for several decades now, so it is hard to grapple with the reality that significant change is happening in the market place today. We are talking micro-marketing and one-on-one customer engagement today. And we are talking about aligning our value propositions with the persons who experience our product. The Principle of Customer Interaction is about making sure that the promised experience matches the delivered experience: the right kiddie toothbrush delivered to the right kid, the right Smart TV delivered to the right family or enthusiast, the right furniture, the right car, the right...

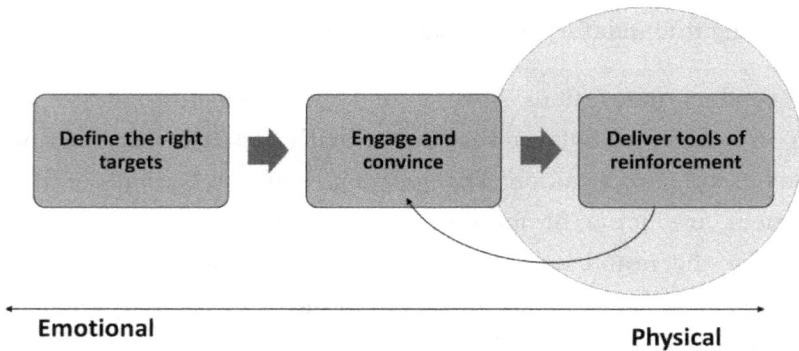

Emotional   **Physical**

Figure 12: The missing link in the interaction spectrum

The question of fit is about how to decide who to target and who to sell to. And as the illustration on the next page highlights, The Principle of Customer Interaction is very much about making the physical experience match the promised one.

1. Define who's the right target or audience

2. Engage and convince
3. Deliver the tools for them to reinforce their choice

You be the judge. How many of your interactions today include a one-two combination punch of both sides of the spectrum? My guess is that they only meet superficially, if at all. Perhaps, the corporate emotional slogans are even ignored by those that actually make and distribute the products because they don't know what to do with them – after all they do have price and schedule constraints. On the other hand, physical experiences are considered as "constraints to tide over" by those defining the emotional connections. And we stick to what is familiar, because convincing all the constituent parts of the entire organization to make the required changes is complex to say the least.

As customers, we are creatures of habit. When we make a change to switch products, we do so either to experiment or because we are now converted to a new belief system. The following cycle illustrates this concept. The cycle has two phases:

1. Experimentation
2. Finalization

The first of the phases is experimentation. When faced with disillusionment, desire to change, desire to explore, or when attracted by the promise of something new, we go through this phase. We typically embark on this journey when the threshold of risk is lowered - whether through social support or pressure, through lower prices or through the ease of coming back to where we started from.

Common examples of experimentation could be:

•   Trying a new brand of bread or yogurt to help us smile at everyone all day
•   Responding to an advertisement for a deodorant that helps men

attract women

- Or when we socially advance to a level when we must have a more sophisticated item such as a car or camera

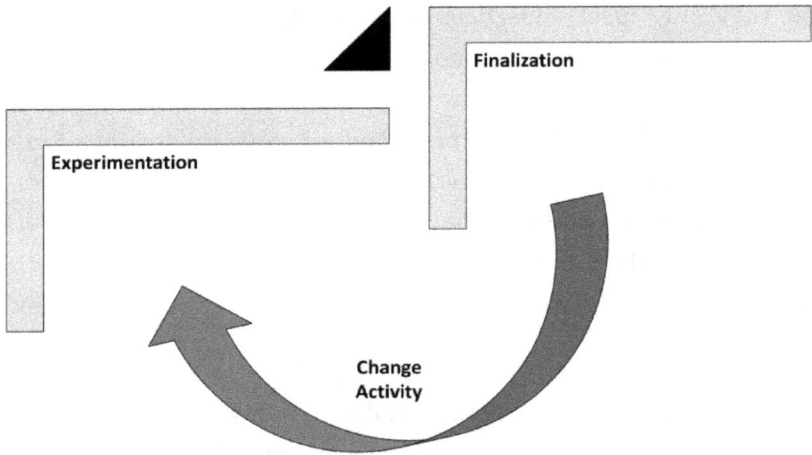

Figure 13: The interaction spectrum and stages of engagement

The second stage is finalization. This is when the decision to change has been made and has been reinforced. The reasons we experimented have been validated and hence we move to the finalization stage.

- We had a pleasant experience with a product or service
- The social reinforcement is strong and complimentary
- The attributes such as value for money, or convenience have been met.

Experimentation and finalization are not absolute stages. Customers frequently move back and forth between the two. Obviously, it's best for business to move a customer to the finalized state as soon as possible, and we must attempt to retain a customer in the finalized state as long as possible. It must also be noted that the duration of time a customer spends in the finalization stage must be completely voluntary and desired. Time spent by the customer because we have made it difficult for them to move back to experimentation through techniques such as long term contracts, burdensome switching etc. are not counted as retention time, even though they may be resulting in revenue or contributing to profits. As we have seen before, every customer we retain through such restrictive means is ultimately a loss to our organization, and especially from the long term intangible perspective.

For firms that have a high interaction index – which have strong and obvious personal interactions with the customer - it is vital to tap into everyday transactions and move up the interaction cycle where the experience is reinforced into satisfaction and then builds into an emotional connection. And for firms that have a low interaction index but high emotional index, strategies to move towards the transactions are crucial to increase stickiness and reduce the effect of promotions.

Emotional barriers are tough to break, but once you allow a chink in the armor, it doesn't take long for a competitor to break through. Physical experiences must support the beliefs from the emotional. We stick to what we have until:

1. We get emotional reinforcement about our negative experiences
2. We get social support for our other choices (recommendations)
3. The risk of change is low (price etc.)
4. Our physical experience with the new choice reinforces our emotional connect

Customers do go back once, just to make sure. But it's all about the right physical reinforcement of the emotional connection, or vice versa. And that's where the moment of truth occurs. If we are able to bring together the physical and the emotional, in that moment of truth, we have a new believer.

| Change Trigger | → | Emotional validation | → | Risk of change evaluation | → | Physical validation | → | Change Initiation |

Figure 14: Capturing the moment of truth in the interaction spectrum

It may be argued that emotional connect is a stronger form of interaction as demonstrated by the most successful brands. After all, once connected at this level, don't customers themselves passionately advocate their brands? However the decision is never of no-return. And The Principle of Customer Interaction is to help you engage customers at both levels to create a sense of exclusivity, pride and security among other things, constantly reinforced every chance they get, to shut out the very thought of entertaining competition.

Emotional connections when also linked to utility as defined by our customers will result in a bond based on both fitment and belonging. As we move from a world of mass marketing to micro-marketing, the potential is immense, and so is the risk of inaction. We must build up both tangible and intangible utility.

1. Tangible utility based on a match with needs and product attributes
2. Intangible utility based on differentiation and aspirational value

3. Tangible and intangible utility based on product superiority (or superiority of what it enables) and aspirational value that it creates.

I mentioned aspirational value above. It is a critical part of market strategy and execution. It is normal for people to aspire. Customers may aspire to meeting some of their tangible personal objectives which are linked to emotional fulfillment, either short or long term in nature.

- Airline loyalty programs are of this nature. They provide a long term aspirational realization by way of an exotic vacation.
- Airline loyalty programs also provide immediate gratification to reinforce value through red carpet treatments, priority boarding etc.

Aspirational value is best realized when it cannot be directly linked to monetary considerations.

Then there are things that we consider more suitable as they move along in life. Often, people attempt to meet their needs with more sophistication and finesse than they did in their prior choices. Whether in business or personal life, the path of evolution will always take place.

- As an example of personal evolution, I used to love (and still do in the mornings) my ceramic cup and instant coffee. Today I use better quality china and better coffee. Tomorrow I might use gourmet coffee made from a really fancy coffee machine, or even brewed more elaborately by investing time.
- On the business end of the spectrum, we look for continuous improvement – better processes, more efficiency, more effectiveness, better software, better collaboration and so on. We forever follow a maturity curve, and as soon as we reach the top

of the curve, something new comes along to start the journey all over again.

It's normal for us to aspire for more depending on social influence, our work environment, our personal interests and many other reasons. Look around us, the examples are everywhere. Right from shoes to computers to cars to pens to t-shirts to window blinds to our oven to our exercise machine to our sofa to that painting on the wall to restaurants. The list is endless.

The way we create customer engagement must cater to these needs and customer segments to set the right expectations. Our identity and position must be clear to our customers. The curve of The Principle of Customer Interaction cycle is based on creating the link between physical attributes and emotional connect. How well are we connecting both of them is the secret to exceptional customer engagement and creating a company that identifies itself with a mission and is galvanized by the zeal to realize it.

The most important takeaway is to remember that survival depends on reflecting our values in terms of customer benefits. After all is said and done, the customers must feel connected and believe that they own something worthwhile if we are to avoid replacement by someone else who makes it happen. For this reason, projecting expertise or quality to the customer gives way to projecting attributes reflected in customer needs and aspirations, like peace of mind, comfort, success, reputation, class, value realized, image, mitigating risk and stability etc. Those attributes must be constantly reinforced − both at the emotional and fulfillment levels. Look at all the successful brands. Most of them are not based on quality, but an attribute of customer aspiration or experience. The Principle of Customer Interaction just works to connect the two ends of the interaction spectrum to create a combination of tangible and intangible utility.

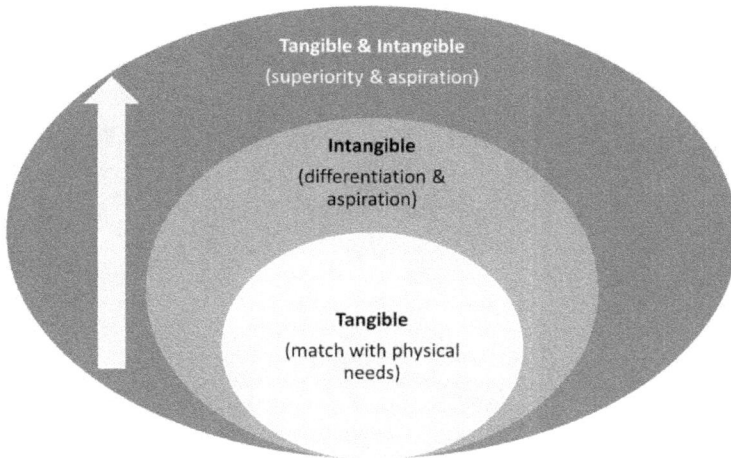

Figure 15: Connecting interaction to utility

More than the transactions themselves, The Principle of Customer Interaction aims to influence the customer at both ends of the cycle to trigger a favorable decision. The underlying factors to control are always differentiation, trust, value, reputation, exclusivity and the tendency to advocate, promote or refer. These are just a few of the customer sentiments we can take as salient examples. How can we define interaction and how can we make The Principle of Customer Interaction work for us? In the next section, we'll address the three steps towards implementing The Principle of Customer Interaction:

1. Understand the current interaction pattern
2. Define the ecosystem around the interaction
3. Establish the strategy to integrate the ecosystem

Implementing the Principle of Customer Interaction

Our customers are interacting with us and our channels today. That's why we are in business. But we are also constantly on the move to retain our existing customers and acquire others to replenish the lost ones. We are constantly innovating to meet emerging needs and expanding our market. In fact, for many businesses, win-back is an important part of the customer acquisition and retention strategy. And this strategy is often based on various types of promotions and offers, an approach that requires elaborate and intricate systems to calculate optimal spend that is based on cost of acquisition and life time value of the customers.

In a digital first world, where collaboration is becoming the norm, innovation and progress today must be thought of with customer experience in mind, whether they are internal users, customers, customer users and partners.

To help us put this in perspective, let's visit the spectrum of interaction that The Principle of Customer Interaction is based on. We'll start with defining:

1. The natural index of customer interaction will indicate where our product or service inherently fits on the interaction curve. As we have discussed earlier, some industries inherently lack physical relationships with their customers and are thus placed on the right hand side of the curve towards the emotional spectrum. Others which are more interactive, or need frequent and direct customer interaction are on the left hand side of the curve.

2. Then we'll try to decode the realized index, or earned index. This is where our product or services actually lie. It measures how we have expanded the interaction and built upon the natural index. The realized index helps understand the state of our current customer engagement. This analysis of the realized index – or

earned index - will give rise to a measure of how we are placed along the spectrum with respect to both physical and emotional engagement. Hopefully, this will result in a visible range on either side of the natural index.

3. The final step will be to review strategies that help expand the range of customer interaction. This is best understood in terms of the interaction range. The broader the interaction range, the better our overall physical and emotional interaction is.

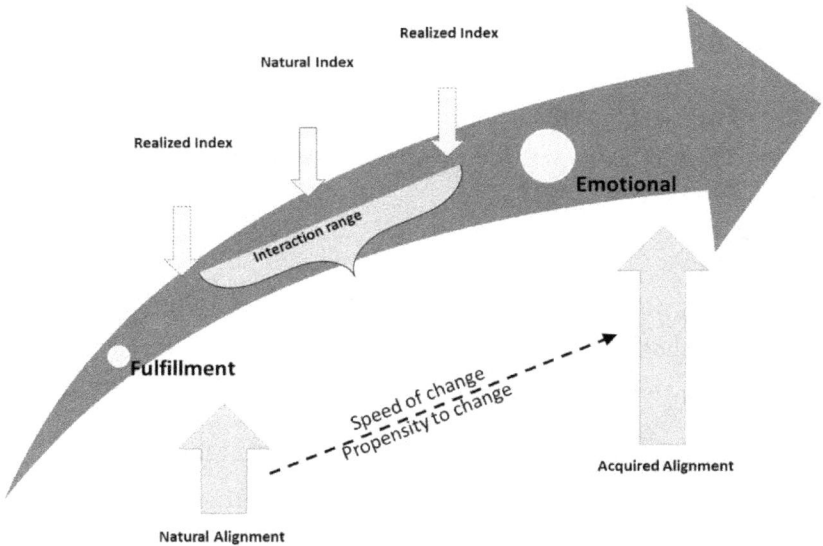

Figure 16: Determining the current interaction model

Table 2: Illustrative parameters to define the natural index

Category	Interaction Measure
Awareness / Marketing	• Do we primarily rely on mass-advertising and promotions to get the word out to create demand? • Do we have records of who our customers and users are?
Distribution	• Do we work with intermediaries who in turn interact with our end customers? • Do we maintain relationships with different stakeholders at different points in the supply or distribution chain? • Are we able to forecast demand based on real consumption levels?
Product development	• Are we generally able to tailor our product or service individually? • Are we able to get granular and direct feedback from customers on what they desire or need in a product?
Customer service	• Do we generally service customers directly or through an intermediary? • Is the customer service data available to other functions?
Sales	• Do customers have avenues to interact with us at an individual level to research their needs and assess fitment with our products?
Customer usage	• Are we generally capable of maintaining individual end customer relationships? Or do we receive aggregated data from our supply chain partners.

For simplicity and understanding, I grouped the parameters into a few different broad categories of engagement. You may come up with more ideas or categories as you analyze your own scenario, but the above list provides a workable starting point. The categories in the table are aligned by some primary functions. The more direct relationship we have with our customers, and the more granular data we have, the better prepared we are bringing the 2 ends of the customer interaction spectrum together.

In short, what is the inherent nature of our industry in general? The next diagram outlines the natural index for a few representative industries.

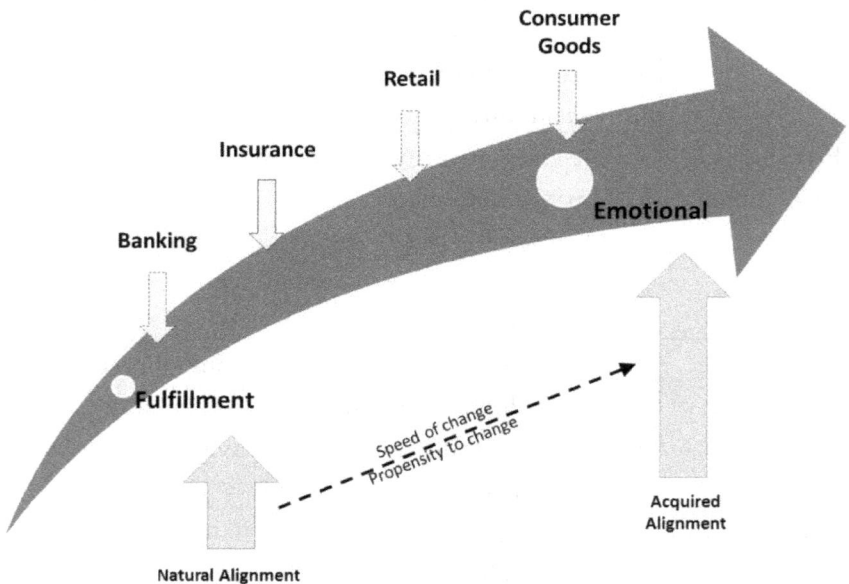

Figure 17: Representative natural index for some industries

Note that while engagement is generally at both ends of the

spectrum, the diagram depicts the most natural placement taking into account how an industry is generally placed.

For those who are more in tune with the 2x2 matrix diagrams will find the next figure more relevant and appealing.

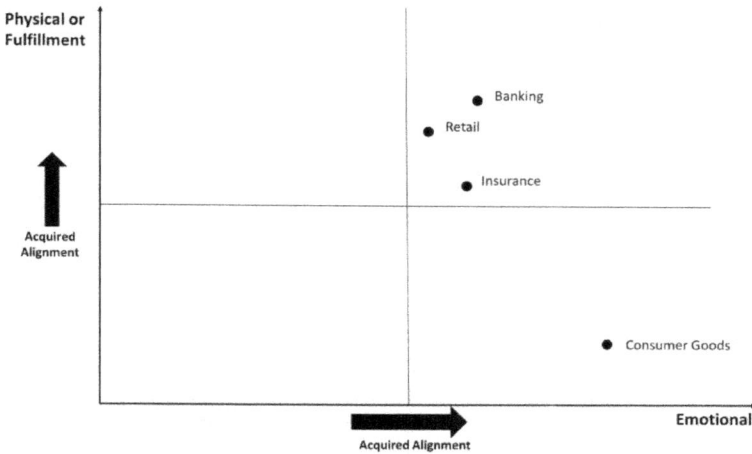

Figure 18: Representative natural index for some industries (2x2 view)

With two measures, emotional and physical, I plotted the industries along the four quadrants. Of course, the top, right hand side box is the way to be in this emerging, digital, social and connected world. Regardless of the way we depict the natural index, it is imperative to both quantitatively and qualitatively define the parameters. The natural index is constantly moving and is dictated by competitive and industry advances. For that reason, plotting our natural index is not an activity that we can perform as we please. In fact for many industries, it's becoming a fight for survival.

Different products and services start at different stages of the interaction spectrum, and the speed and propensity to engage with the customers is often dictated by their inherent position in the spectrum. As we will see by the parameters that measure the natural index, it is sometimes easier to advance more quickly towards the emotional end of the spectrum than trying to build up missing interaction towards the physical end of the spectrum.

Industries whose index is naturally aligned to the fulfillment end of the spectrum may have an inherent advantage in the play for customer engagement. Their position implies that they can use the tools for emotional engagement and branding, in addition to also effectively engaging at the fulfillment level. As an example, consider that banking customers interact with the product everyday through transactions and loyalty programs, while they are also influenced by the branding strategies of the bank. These industries have the capability to maintain - and leverage actively - direct and intimate customer relationships.

On the other hand, consumer product manufacturers for example, play primarily on the emotional end of the spectrum to manage demand. They must go through business intermediaries such as distributors but must ultimately own the efforts to ensure that demand for their products stays high with respect to competition. In a model like that, they must give up some control on customer experience. Such industries on the higher end of the curve may be considered to have an inherent disadvantage as far as customer interaction is concerned. They must make additional efforts to engage customers at the physical level.

Now let's examine how we can plan our customer interaction and engagement strategies to maximize the interaction range. That is what really matters.

To ensure that the emotional and fulfillment ends of the spectrum are both firing and aligned with each other, there is a need to understand the following two aspects, working in tandem with each other. Bringing the two ends of the customer interaction curve together creates lasting advantages both in terms of strengthening customer engagement and building barriers to entry for competitors. Both of these have tangible benefits in terms of customer satisfaction and retention.

The first question to ask is: what meaningful positions would you want to create in the customer's mind?

In a digital world, the barriers to becoming undifferentiated are very low. The amount of communication and messaging delivered to customers is immense. And while it seems to works for a while, it quickly starts boiling down to promotions in case of consumer products, and services reinforcement for more complex products. It may seem that in many cases we don't have anything unique to offer our customers, but that is only a perception in our own minds. Customer will always have us pegged somewhere in their mind, once we get there, of course. There is generally a combination of factors customers evaluate and compare us against such as affordability, prestige, reliability, belonging, comfort of working together, cultural alignment etc.

We'll examine this concept of uniqueness and differentiation in the chapter on The Principle of Un-Commoditization. Until then, the most important activity is to determine the values and message we would like to project. For business-business industries the keys lie in aligning with the overall business ecosystem that our customers are trying to build and aspiring towards. For consumer oriented industries, opening direct communication channels with consumers is the way to go. As we will see in chapters on The Principle of Presenting and The Principle of Completion, these are not difficult endeavors if approached from a framework of engaging more comprehensively along both ends of the spectrum (along both axes of the 2x2 matrix). The underlying force is that we create messages that can be translated to, and reinforced by engagement at the physical level.

The second question to ask is: what kind of fulfillment mechanisms can we use to reinforce the emotional connections?

This is where the interaction range really starts to broaden. How does every customer touch-point reinforce the emotional end of the spectrum? Even if we are not equipped to identify individual customers, we still have several excellent avenues for engagement. Advances in social media integration, customer communities, connected devices, and consumer centric capabilities such as mobile and geo location are beginning to provide the tools to achieve this.

Some foundational capabilities to think of are:

- Identifying customers individually and creating avenues for personal interaction
- Maintained and acting upon granular transaction and interaction pattern information
- More granularly segmenting and analyzing the effects of engagement strategies
- For the most part, not relying on intermediaries – or perhaps strongly influencing intermediaries - to define the customer experience on our behalf

Ultimately, The Principle of Customer Interaction becomes a fight for maintaining the customer interface. It's easy to see the difficulties that are being faced by all types of industries today. Rather than giving up control, the right approach is to get our share of the customer interface and influence the customer experience in a meaningful way. If we give up control, we face the risk of being anonymous fulfillment providers – or fulfillment providers with a name – which is not a pretty place to be in within today's connected world. We only have to look at the immense change in the consumer banking and payments landscape where giving up the customer interface has led to a fight for survival of the business model itself. Regulatory and other such constraints will only serve to slow the movement, but not stop it. The rise of the niches in all categories of products will ultimately be decided by who gets to reinforce their value in front of customers every day, whether its food, software, durables or professional services.

In the previous chapter, The Principle of External Reinforcement provided the foundation of how to partner with customers and be engaged in their decision cycle or journey. In this chapter we saw how The Principle of Customer Interaction provides the foundation for creating effective interaction at both physical and emotional ends of the customer engagement spectrum.

In my view the easiest way to embark on this journey is to think about it as a model that allows us to benchmark our progress and status against the goals we set. Our competition, the perceptions of our customers, the way we define our business processes and the performance of our products are all aspects that feed into the model. In fact, for each component in the model, we should set qualitative and quantitative criteria that provide an unbiased – and sometimes – not so flattering scorecard of how we are doing in the marketplace.

A checklist to assess our current levels will serve to explain the concept of how to expand our interaction range.

☐ When do customers interact with us (pre-purchase, sales, service, operations)?
☐ How frequent is the interaction?

☐ Who do the customers interact with?

☐ Why do customers interact with us?

☐ Can customers switch easily?

☐ What are some common drivers for switching?

☐ How frequently do users consume the information you give them?

☐ What are the methods by which they interact with us?

☐ Where do they interact with us?

☐ What is the level of emotional connection they can have with us?

☐ Do the avenues to interact with each other? As a community?

☐ Are we building methods to engage in those communities?

☐ Can we interact with customers based on context (where they are, who they are, which life stage they are in)?

For each parameter we must think of three dimensions:

1. The potential level of performance; dictated by what our competitors are doing, how our partners are engaging and the innovations that are threatening to disrupt the model we are used to. For example, retailers and distributors could be creating avenues of engagement that perhaps a product manufacturer can boost? Perhaps customers themselves are providing hints on how they would like to buy our industrial products, and consume information?

2. Actual performance; dictated by an honest assessment of our status. Sometimes the right initiatives fail for a variety of reasons. And more often than not, failures lie in how the customers are expected to engage. For example, providing coupons on our mobile app is great, but if customers can't use them in context, the adoption curve will be slow. For the purposes of this chapter, our assessment is on how well we are interacting across both ends of the interaction spectrum. A direct

indicator of that are the links we have created, or are planning to create, between the physical and emotional ends of the spectrum. They must complement each other.

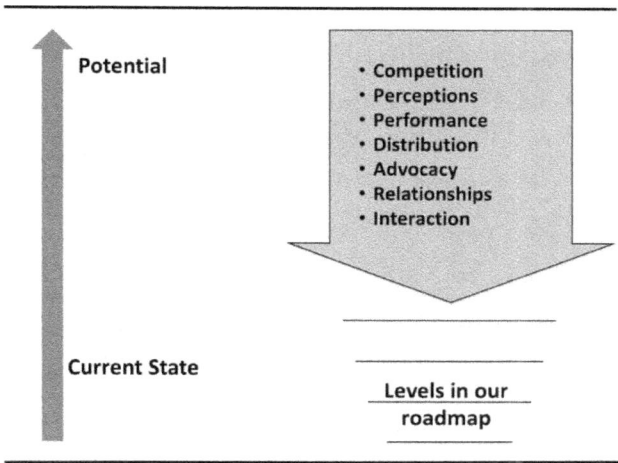

Figure 19: Incremental roadmap towards expanding the interaction range

3. A roadmap to reduce the gap between actual and potential performance; this is a journey filled with both possibilities and constraints. There is so much to do, and yet we have limitations on what we can do in a given amount of time. The best way is to understand the major developments in the industry that will influence future trends. Deriving conclusions from that is the single most important piece of the puzzle that causes tremendous disruption in the market. We have witnessed spectacular failures recently because companies failed to innovate fast enough. Don't discount the developments in the market. Don't resist them. Study them and think of how you would like to evolve. The purpose of our business is not our product, but what it was meant to solve. And if that purpose is being met by alternate means, we

must absolutely evolve & align with that. We do need to keep in mind short term market needs to both acquire and retain customers. The benchmark model and vision will be a good validator of the choices we are making.

Understanding and applying The Principle of Customer Interaction requires determining the inherent characteristics of our business, and expanding the interaction range to reach and engage our customers much more comprehensively. It is the only way to engage in the digital world.

3

The Principle of Un-Commoditization

Creating points of un-commoditization allows us to establish relationships that build on that proposition, and that drives our entire product, corporate and marketing strategy. Un-commoditization is not an add-on.

Un-Commoditization is an often talked about and hotly debated topic. I chose to include The Principle of Un-Commoditization as an integral part of the five principles. Note that I am not calling it differentiation because the word differentiation is so often used that it has become a product focused subject, and doesn't drive home the dire consequences of missing the bus on customer engagement in today's digital world. Creating points of un-commoditization allows us to establish relationships that build on that proposition, and that drives our entire product, corporate and marketing strategy. Un-commoditization is not an add-on, or we'll be forever talking about it without really achieving it. It's baked in with our core vision, our company's DNA and how our organization operates, collaborates and grows.

How many times have we heard someone say "We are in a commodity market; times are getting tough and we can't differentiate"? This, despite the widely known methods such as creating products of varying quality and price (think of a vertical ladder of product variants), and different horizontal variants of the same product (think of different flavors of ice-cream).

Hence, it is important to understand that un-commoditization is not the same as segmentation or a niche. We may produce high quality, high priced products that are essentially the same as those of our competitors in the same space. Instead, un-commoditization begins with defining our purpose, not our current products or service lines. Then it germinates in the mind of the customer and is nurtured. It must be constantly reinforced, demonstrated through proof points, and complemented by what they perceive when they interact with us. The other four principles will be actively used to support the points of un-commoditization. As we evolve, this process repeats. In today's world, no one can restrict our access to customers and un-commoditization is always possible. Un-commoditization simply means that we do something differently that our customers can relate to and appreciate. Un-commoditization is imperative because it helps the customers to:

1. Defend their choice
2. Promote their choice and
3. Feel good about their choice

This chapter provides a solid framework to help us begin to execute this critical prerequisite for our business. The factors for un-commoditization may be of various types. The important thing is to have one, and to make sure it is meaningful to our customers. As we will explore in this chapter, Un-commoditization is often iterative – or an upward spiral - and it fuels its own momentum by charting the way for subsequent innovation.

We start with a simple value proposition built on our purpose, and as we go along, new possibilities to serve that purpose are discovered. Aligning with purpose and perhaps even watching it evolve is important because it allows us to uncover adjacencies in our business we would otherwise never think about. These adjacencies can either pave the way for growth or allow in competitors who will take away our advantages.

- Can we call Salesforce.com a CRM product company today? Instead it has evolved into a platform provider for a connected enterprise.
- Can we call Apple a manufacturer of phones? We definitely can but we'll only be describing half of the company's story.
- The luxury brands we love have evolved to meet so many different needs in the personal space.

In the chapter on Principle of Customer Interaction, we delved deeper into how the two ends of the interaction spectrum work together and feed into each other. In this chapter we will analyze the mechanics of effective un-commoditization. I will reiterate that un-commoditization should be meaningful to customers, it must be tied to purpose, it must guide internal operations and it must be constantly reinforced by interacting on both ends of the customer interaction spectrum.

Real un-commoditization can be either tangible or intangible.

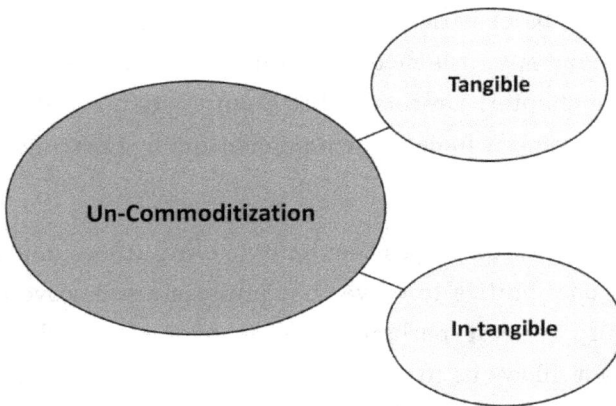

Figure 20: The two types of un-commoditization

Tangible is when our products are different, and intangible is when the customer "feels" the difference, although the underlying products may really be the same. Both kinds of un-commoditization will work together to create the total value proposition. If we were to ask what un-commoditization means, here's a simple checklist to fill out:

☐ There is a clear link to how it benefits or relates to the target customer segments

☐ It can be executed and sustained well by the organization's operational processes (aligned to purpose and DNA)

☐ It's easy to convey to the target segment (marketing and sales)

☐ Not many others can claim the same because we can constantly build on it to raise barriers (uniqueness)

☐ It won't limit future plans on product line or geography expansions (growth and evolution)

☐ It links all our products together so that value propositions are integrated (aligned to purpose)

Let's look at each of these in detail:

1. There is a clear link to how it benefits or relates to the target customer segments

If we claim something about our business or our product, it's obvious that it must clearly tie in with why it matters for our customers. Being locally run, sourcing our raw material from a particular region, following a certain customer service philosophy, a business process that is customized, simplifying technology, allowing faster time to market to clients, being exclusive, being prestigious, being highest quality, providing better access – all of these may or may not matter directly to customers who do business with us. We could be different when we think about who we are, but we may still be the same as others in our customers' eyes. If our points of differentiation don't matter to our customers, or if they don't know how it matters to them, then it's an empty and wasted slogan. We must find a direct and quantifiable link between our values and our customers. For example:

- For services businesses, the slogan "we care for you" should reflect in how they engage. The slogan must flow down to the physical end of the customer interaction spectrum

- For a community bank, how should the slogan "we have deep ties with the community" connect with its day-to-day interactions with customers?

- For luxury brands, how does exclusivity and high quality make them non-interchangeable with the others in the same category? Is there something that is uniquely them?

Consider Starbucks. "We pick the best beans" now reflects in the coffee and the environment they serve. They've gone from "what an expensive cup of coffee!" to being a synonym for an excellent coffee experience.

Consider the world's largest technology product companies. They are demonstrating every day to enterprises how they are integrating better and enabling a better return on investment or time to market.

Un-commoditization is integrally linked with the rest of the principles. For example, think again about The Principle of Customer Interaction. All of the companies who push the un-commoditization agenda successfully are able to engage well at both the physical and emotional ends of the spectrum. In short they are consistent in their positioning and in their demonstration of the quoted un-commoditization. Their points of un-commoditization are linked to the way they connect and interact with customers. And by being consistent, the differentiation percolates throughout the organization to increase focus and continuous reinforcement. And hence the un-commoditization comes out strongly and uniquely when we speak about these companies. Whether it's Wal-Mart and its everyday low prices, Apple with its user experience principles, or Vanguard with its no active management philosophy resulting in low expense ratios for investors, these companies are indeed constantly evolving and changing, but the foundation of their differentiation has been the same.

2. It's easy to convey to the target customer segments

Un-commoditization should be easy to relay. Consider terms like excellent customer service, culture of innovation, or a passion for making a difference. How can we make the un-commoditization more tangible so that customers instantly know what you mean, rather than wonder what you mean? When retailers or banks talk about customer service, what do they mean?

Once we identify our point of differentiation, we should be able to simplify it and make it so specific that it is easily understandable. In the absence of that, customers will wonder about it and never really get it. When that happens, un-commoditization efforts are wasted. We might feel excited talking about it inside the organization, but our customers don't feel the same. Most organizations that operate at the emotional end of the customer interaction spectrum risk falling into this category. They operate in a niche – prestige, high quality etc. - but within the niche they are interchangeable. The same is true of organizations that execute well at the physical end of the spectrum – retailers or banks – but primarily compete on variables such as price promotions to engage customers. The essence is in deviating from the median path and taking a polarizing stand, whether that stems from unique product assortments or customer segments. This polarizing stand is then reinforced at both the emotional and physical ends of the customer interaction spectrum. We'll discuss polarization later in this chapter.

- Organizations that deal with products that they don't manufacture often rely on non-product differentiators. Since these organizations don't control the quality of the product, claiming product supremacy is a un-commoditization that can easily be copied. Hence the un-commoditization must come from non-product attributes. Positioning an expert image that helps customer adoption and use of the products is an example. The expert value could arise from creating additional complimentary services around the core product to gain a leg up on the competition, providing advisory services, or offering a model that guarantees satisfaction.

- Organizations that make products must focus on product un-commoditization in terms of an attribute of the product's value proposition that they can call their own. Quality and price differentiators are easiest to claim but are often like a curve function. The perception of quality and price is up to the customer segment that interacts with us and pays for our products. Sacrificing some attributes while making a move to own others builds polarization among the players. The resulting approach leads to a positioning that is aligned with customer needs (peace, comfort, ego, saves time, etc.).

3. Not many others can claim the same (ideally none)

Your customers will always ask, "How are you different from x?" They ask this question as they consider your product and compare it to the competition. Knowing that truth is enough for us to begin preparing for this question and reinforce it every chance we get. Otherwise, it doesn't matter how highly we think of our brand, if we cannot answer this question, we are replaceable. Sometimes, it may be easy for us because our competition may not be operating in our territory yet, or the customer may not be thinking about them, but we can't depend on that forever. We must continue to create and emphasize the points of un-commoditization.

Even luxury brands and consumer brand companies can't get away without this. Even though they have the "quality" and "image" differentiators, they are still engaged in price and promotion wars with their few competitors. When we are fighting for mass reach, that's an outcome to be expected; but it would be great to have a niche that's just ours. Price promotions may be inevitable given the deal seeking nature of humans, but it doesn't have to be the only way to get customers. It's about owning a sentiment in the customer's mind that can just be attributed to us, not to everyone else who's like us. That attribute drives the foundation of un-commoditization and aligns the rest of the organization – people, operations, marketing, customer service and others – around it.

4. It can be executed and sustained well (operational processes)

Un-commoditization cannot be superficial, because that won't matter in the long run. Customers must see a "proof point." To be driven home, un-commoditization must be supported by our marketing, our messaging, our product, our service, and everything that touches the customer. We need to assess our claims, map the proof points and then demonstrate how we will deliver on the claims. The proof points should be delivered by demonstrating tangible items that make up the un-commoditization.

- A manufacturing company may tout exceptional quality. Do they have better quality processes? Better audits? Have their products passed tests that others have failed? How will they keep it up? Is there a checklist they provide to their clients? Do they provide a real guarantee of certain items that indeed point to a differentiated offering?

- A services company may tout better access to senior management. First, will that be demonstrated by in-person meetings or events? And then, will that bring better quality, better innovation, or faster time to market? How? In short, how will it matter to customers?

- An e-commerce firm may tout excellent service. Will they reduce customer anxiety regarding returns? Easier pick-ups? Real time tracking? Returns made simple? Transparency in refund amounts? Communication to supplier? Anonymous feedback?

- A luxury brand may promise exclusivity and a unique style that screams their brand to the people in the know. Are they delivering on that promise consistently or through specially orchestrated and occasional campaigns?

The key is to create tangible un-commoditization where we can continue to build a reputation. Even as our differentiators are copied (which they obviously will be), a relentless focus creates an organizational culture that provides us with the fuel to keep innovating. It's not easy to keep up with organizations that can accomplish this. Most customers may not need to "really use" our un-commoditization. They just need to know it exists and it's real, because they'll experience it when the need arises, and will advocate for us over our competition when that happens. Isn't that the holy-grail our business is seeking to achieve?

5. It won't limit future plans on product line or geography expansions

This is an important and often misunderstood parameter primarily because of the similarity with branding and brand extensions. In most cases, over time our brand will be built through our performance – messaging, perceptions, price, quality, service, etc. And there always comes a time when we grow bigger, our customer segment changes, or our original geographic boundaries evolve. It seems to be that what may have appealed to our smaller customers or to our local customers may not appeal to the bigger customers or those in a different region.

But that's a myth. I call this confusion "The loss of the founder's passion." If what we have doesn't appeal to the segment anymore, then where is our core un-commoditization? What most companies do is dump the great thing they have, and try to copy their competitors. And then they get lost in the shuffle. They become just another drop in the bucket.

Staying true to our brand values is the key. Being Japanese sells all over the world because these companies stick to their core proposition of reliability no matter what else they do. In fact they have failed when they've let go of that foundation. I recently experienced a high end apparel brand selling in most stores at an unbelievably low price. After researching the brand, I found that they are going "wider". The overall sales for the company are indeed greater than before. But my "bargain" was not really a bargain because I didn't value it highly anymore. Their customer segment has changed, or that's the signal they sent out.

Our positioning may not be for everyone, but that's exactly what is intended. People will tell you name matters. What matters most is identifying the right place for our brand in the customers' minds. As we will see in the Principle of Presenting, the only thing to be careful of is to make sure our positioning does not close the doors to the adjacencies in our business.

6. It links all our products together so that value propositions are integrated

This last item may appear to be a little surprising, but it is the mainstay of how we operate in the digital economy. In the modern digital economy, the biggest un-commoditization could very well be that we don't define our strategy and customer experience by product, geography or any other such classification. Instead we think of the total customer ecosystem and stack our offerings according to the needs spectrum, and make conscious choices about the gaps that remain. Here, more than the product, the un-commoditization of our organization's philosophy comes into play, and then percolates down to the products. An organization is always built with a passion, to address a need. If we have multiple products or business lines, it's always a good idea to put them to the test of the organization's philosophy.

- For example, Vanguard, an investment house, pushes "value". Its claim is that the auto pilot investments that track the key market indices do as well or even better than the funds that have an active asset manager. Hence, the expense ratio of its funds - the commission the fund house charges you – are significantly less than that of actively managed funds. That one key un-commoditization permeates the offerings even as customers are given other options that don't resonate with this belief. Vanguard's value proposition is always clear. They make it easy for you to follow that chain of thought and provide a good interface to help you invest. Vanguard puts its money where its mouth is by providing enough proof points to establish its value proposition as the ultimate truth that eludes many smart people.

- On the other hand, think about a consumer bank. All of us have one. Visit their website or their branch. The bank does not really know you as a customer, just as a user of one of their products or services. When they sell, they sell a product, not address a need that is real to you. Imagine what would happen, if they were to say, "you've just graduated college, start thinking of your retirement. We don't have an offering in that area but go to Vanguard.com and open an IRA. Here's why. And use this credit card that will automatically earn points for you to send to your savings account. And we have a dashboard that shows if you are managing your income and spending wisely. And never use your credit card to carry balances. If you ever need to stretch, call me and we'll plan it together." But we are always selling either a card or bank accounts or another service. Customers never get to experience the bank, only a part of it. The same can be said of a majority of businesses.

It must be noted that un-commoditization and a niche are two different beasts. By doing more in fewer areas, we can achieve specialization and expertise, but we must still take specific steps to differentiate ourselves in this more narrowly defined market. Operating in a niche is a strategic choice that depends on several factors we won't discuss in a lot of detail in this book. But whatever our niche, chances are that we won't be the only one for too long. Hence it is important to create those un-commoditization factors that address the all-important question – why should I choose you over others?

Why We Need Un-Commoditization Early

By telling our customers that we are just another choice to consider, we may survive, but will likely not thrive. This is because while it may seem like a good choice to grow as our market grows, soon, without well-defined differentiating factors, the competition heats up and it becomes harder to play the game. Prices start falling, expenses begin to grow, products start to merge in terms of their quality and customers begin to treat our category as a commodity.

The normal response to the increased competitive activity is then to build the un-commoditization factors. Experience and scale of our operations may help to keep us afloat, but the built up inertia and culture resist the change. The ultimate result is that the organization must go through a reorganization to reinvent itself on many fronts – customer perception, people, skills, marketing strategy, sales approach and of course the overall culture. Not many companies have survived this, and it becomes a long, arduous journey. The earlier we start, the better our prospects.

Un-commoditization is not an add-on. It's not about marketing and how we advertise. Rather, it's about our philosophy and our purpose. It then percolates down to functions such as product development, research, marketing, sales, distribution, people, vendor management and almost all aspects of our value chain. In order to really differentiate, organizational culture in all quarters must be aligned. For that alignment to come true, the passion for the cause must be kindled. And passion doesn't come through window dressing, just as culture doesn't change through slogans. Unless it is clear to the leaders how they want to play, our value proposition will appear disjointed and broken to our customers. For firms that just want to play and catch what is thrown their way, this approach may work. For those who aspire to be significant to their customers, and create a true partnership for mutual benefits, and return greater shareholder wealth, it's crucial that the un-commoditization platform be defined and navigated throughout the organization.

The approaches to effective un-commoditization can be categorized as follows. There are numerous variations of course but these categories serve as a good baseline. We'll review each of the above in the following sections.

Table 3: Categories of un-commoditization

Category of Un-commoditization	What it Implies
Model Expansion	Building adjacent capabilities to support our core value proposition to enhance stickiness and expertise
Polarizing	Addressing a set of customer segments at the risk of others shunning us
Aspirational	Being the "next level when they are ready" in the customer's mind. Must be combined with other levers to truly differentiate within this category
Intrinsic	Meeting a new or unique need in the market place. Must be combined with other levers to sustain this position

1.   Un-commoditization Through Expanding our Model

Customers almost always have a need spectrum that is wider than what we offer. Traditionally, expansion has been used to address new segments. In the context of our discussion, the expansion is from the customer's perspective. What else can we do that will make our value proposition more attractive to customers? As simple as it sounds, not many can go beyond their core service offering, or beyond launching new products and geographies. Following model expansion has many organizational challenges such as understanding of the space, current brand image and established operating models such a channel management. Adjacencies often make product and service offerings much more attractive and introduce high levels of client stickiness and avenues for more comprehensive customer engagement. Such a model is especially attractive if customers are struggling with many different isolated activities in the food chain.

When there is failure to expand the model, it results in the value proposition becoming commoditized. If we provide value to clients, we must also make it easier for clients to prove the return on their investments. More so if the value delivered is directly linked to how well clients work with other parts of the food chain.

- Think of Salesforce.com. We thought of them as a CRM. Then they offered products for customer service and marketing. Their evolution had already secured them the user interface. And now they are on the cusp of organizing themselves as a connected enterprise platform company, bringing the entire enterprise to their customers. Suddenly it's much more attractive for enterprises to do so.

- All of our favorite brands have followed the same expansion model by offering more and more consumer products that are linked together. Most well-known apparel brands started out with a single product category, and leveraged their brand promise to expand into other categories.

It's often difficult for incumbents to see how their industry is changing, and how their un-commoditization needs to evolve.

- Take the example of sales and marketing agencies. One type of agency calls potential customers, pitches their clients' products and helps set up sales meetings. In order to engage and nurture these customers, their clients adopt thought leadership vehicles, sponsor events and perform detailed segmentation of their prospects. Despite the emerging B2B sales models that call for more tightly integrated sales and marketing efforts, many of these agencies do not think beyond their core model. Adopting inbound marketing principles or a multi-channel approach to build their own audience and nurture the customers could have been an appealing option, but very few get around to putting themselves in the customers' shoes to actually consider the shift. More contacts, more types of campaigns, more geographic regions and more industries – fighting a war based on perceived differentiators and waiting for someone else to pull the rug from under their feet.

This is not specific to any one industry. These companies need to devote a little think time and look at themselves from the outside in. That changes the perspective.

- Think about logistics providers. The most dominant ones are great companies who have created several barriers to entry for their businesses. But they still have the same make a package, hand it over and track it model. What can be done to engage with customers in addition to remaining an invisible, seamless provider of services. The trends are obvious in how the industry is evolving. Amazon's grocery distribution network and the ship-to-store model being followed by retailers are disruptions waiting for new local players to come on board. It's true, a Wal-Mart package can be picked up from a designated location and that may work for some consumers. But does it align with the expanding online shopping habits, the community based sentiments, real time shipping and ship-to-store needs. For example, when our home directly begins to order stuff by itself (yes, that's coming), will other players like service technicians enter the distribution market? How are the big players preparing to tackle the changing landscape?

Expanding a model is a difficult change. But it's likely to be what will define a winner in this connected economy. Barriers between industries and models are falling every day, and we must be ready to march through them, instead of giving them up to someone else.

2. Un-Commoditization Can Be Polarizing

Positioning, company strategy and marketing are all about sentimental and targeted share of mind. It must be noted that un-commoditization segments and divides our market. It makes our overall market smaller but much more relevant. If we say we are different from someone else, then we challenge the individual customer or group to make an explicit choice of either selecting us or our competitors. The immediate choices may be dependent on several factors such as price and convenience (which may or may not be a market opportunity for us based on our strategy), but for those in our defined target segment and sweet spot, the cross roads are obvious. Customers must make a choice, and the more often they choose, the more opportunities we have to cement our relationships. Polarization can make choices easier for customers. Polarization will reduce our total market size, but it makes that smaller market much more attractive than a larger, more general one.

The way to cater to a larger market is by creating more than one differentiated brands or offerings, not creating one-size-fits-all products. Trying to be everything takes us down the path of being commoditized, and that's the first sign that our longevity as a business is at stake. When customers ask the question "Why did we choose them", they may not find a robust answer to defend their choice. In fact, inertia may be the only answer they come up with. That's a dangerous state to be in.

The effect of polarization, though apparently threatening to our empire building goals, is desirable and very powerful. It galvanizes our organization, focuses our value proposition and rallies everyone around a common agenda. But if our goals are only linked to size or magnitude, then the polarizing effects can be countered by adopting proven branding strategies that create un-commoditization, instead of diluting our identify. Trying to ride two boats at the same time is dangerous. We must make a choice – spread or differentiate. That's why Nike doesn't focus on office attire, McKinsey focuses on management advisory, and that's why Pizza Hut and Taco Bell are two different Yum! Brands. Polarization is about our ownership of an attribute of our product or service, sustained creation of competitive entry barriers and a complete alignment of our entire organizational value chain. When the market thinks of that attribute, they think about us, and we are in an exclusive position to deliver on that attribute, over and over again.

- Consider German car makers. They were known for quality, class and performance. Over time their expertise expanded to other customer segments as well. Expanding customer segments brings in new dimensions of service, price and customer experiences. These must be handled delicately without diluting the brand image and promise across other customer segments. There are inherent differences between buyers who buy for performance and prestige, versus those that buy for practicality and long term cost of ownership.

A strategy based on polarization is effective but difficult to consistently execute. It requires the courage to continue to operate by our claims and not let the brand be diluted by straying from its original path. The biggest enemy of polarization is greed – greed for short cuts to short-term results and greed for general world domination. Marketing alone does not change perceptions. Un-commoditization is an organizational initiative. If all parts are not in sync, people can see through the thin shell.

3. Un-Commoditization Can Be Aspirational

Un-commoditization is about creating an emotional position based on careful engineering of the underlying product. Fear, trust, pride, exclusivity, belonging and association are all factors for creating an emotional connection. We may overlook the lack of physical un-commoditization when we feel an emotional connection.

As we plan our strategy and positioning, it is worth keeping in mind that un-commoditization based on aspirations has the following inherent risks we must mitigate or resolve:

• Changing social preferences
• Generational differences

With the passage of time, certain societal values change. For example, as a society we've become more eco-conscious in the past decade. The customer segment that cared deeply about recycling is expanding. The influence is expanding beyond a niche and is becoming a more broadly accepted function. This trend has no doubt been accelerated by rising fuel and commodity prices. Smaller cars are marketed under the positioning of being zippy, convenient and offering drivers a choice to "be different". And the "be different" positioning is taking on local dimensions as well. Entire cities are being stereotyped with certain behaviors. Top 10 lists for ecofriendly cities are popping up all over. And as Nike found out, we are much more aware of whether factories that make the products we love are doing so in a humane manner.

Another trend worth noting is of shunning what was previously considered classy. More and more people are returning to a lifestyle more suited to the faster pace of life. Style and elegance are being replaced by honesty and self-esteem. Marketing yourself as such is en vogue, and the rise of social media and channels like Twitter, YouTube, blogs, and Facebook are fueling that trend. And what's the best way to gain attention other than being different from the rest, or following folks who manage to do so quickly?

The framework on the next page helps to define some considerations. The criteria to consider are broad. Look at the table to examine which social preferences and beliefs are changing and how they will influence our un-commoditization.

As customers, we are becoming more accustomed to social and multi-channel. In fact, it is a way to show that we are the "new" generation. We follow celebrities who influence how we think, and we openly tell everyone what we thought of something or what we liked. We are also becoming more global in our thinking and more aware of core values and behaviors that other countries bring to the marketplace. We are more acutely aware of economic impacts that global trade has on local economies. For example, after the recent financial crisis, anything that brings US jobs back is in demand.

Table 4: A framework to evaluate changing social preferences and their impact on our un-commoditization

Cause	What is changing?	Segments it affects	Risks to mitigate	Opportunities to tap into
Political / economic				
Environmental e.g. Go green				
Health e.g. Go organic				
Style				
Financial e.g. Go OpEx versus CapEx				
Attitude influencers e.g. maturity of product/ service area				
Hobbies				
Others				

Our un-commoditization must stand the test of time or adapt to the change. No trend is forever. Time has shown that these are all cyclic in nature. The fact is that our need to be different keeps us shuttling between trends. What is niche today will become main-stream tomorrow and vice versa. The speed of change is dictated by economic realities.

Now let's take a look at generational differences.

There are experts out there who make these predictions for a living so I'll play safe and just outline the framework for some self-service.

Table 5: A framework to evaluate generational triggers and their impact on our un-commoditization

Generational Triggers	Description
Revolt	Has our product become an accepted way of life? The revolt will be on what our product stands for today.
Convenience	The next generation needs shortcuts. What out there is making it easy for them? They'll go back to adopting complex stuff, of course.
Novelty	As in "let's ring in the new and transform the way we do stuff."
Return to basics	As in disillusionment "we don't know where we are going. Let's take stock and start fresh with the basics."
Self service	As in "I need to be more independent. Give me self service capabilities." Of course the next generation will want someone else to do it for them behind the scenes.

We are a species that has at its core the desire to be different. We revolt. We want to make the same mistakes our parents made instead of learning from them. In a new job, we want to change what exists so we can put our own stamp on the future. From that arises cycles of trends. Because of this, for many products, it is safe to assume that certain practices and styles will be rejected by the next generation but eventually may come back in full force with the following generation. Generational effects could be natural (15-20 years) or corporate (3-5 years).

A few years ago I loved my brand of sports shoes. I identified with them. I showed them off when I had to make a statement and identify with the brand community. Now, I am brand agnostic. I want to "de-brand" myself. At least for my "searching-for-an-un-commoditization- factor" brain, the leading sports brands do not have what I want. They compete for the same place in my mind. Any un-commoditization in this case is created by our perception shaped by advertising and the social circles we're in. So the exact opposite attributes are behind my current de-branding philosophy – go local, be nature friendly and be different. I'm sure I'll be back as more people become like me, and I find a reason to be different again.

And that's that. We love to be different. Either we adopt from the new generation to show we are different from our current one, or we reject the new because we want to show how the old is golden. My professor at school used to say, "When we change our identity, we must fanatically reject our previous one to protect what we have adopted new." I find it true universally. Whether it's changing countries, changing fashions, changing religions, changing brand; we must reject the old, or at least appear to do so. Nowhere is it more relevant than generational and social differences.

4.   Un-Commoditization Can be Universal but Intrinsic
Then there is un-commoditization that is universal but truly different. There are very few that offer what you can offer. Passage of time implies experience which in turn implies innovation which in turn implies more maturity and quality. Companies that manage to do this succeed because with every passing day they and their customers enhance the barriers to entry for others – investments, supply chain, data, knowledge, top place in the customers' minds

among others.

Consider Amazon, Apple or Google. What's so special about them? The inherent genius they had can be copied but it hasn't been. And these firms keep changing, constantly evolving and innovating to enhance the barriers to entry. What would you copy even if you decide you wanted to? Each passing day raises a new barrier.

- Google has gone from being a search engine to being a generator of information that is only available on Google networks. They have leveraged that to make forays into commerce. Their mobile initiatives are geared to create even more context by generating more personalized information.

- Similarly, Amazon went from being an online book store to the biggest online warehouse. And it's still evolving. Amazon evolves every day to protect its core business, and you can't be sure what its core business is today. From television to media to e-book readers to reseller networks to marketplaces to distribution partner to payments – can you really define Amazon and its biggest competitor today?

- Apple is moving from being a genius device maker to being the payments facilitator of the world. The company's new Apple Watch is a foray into the exciting but uncharted territory of remote sensing and personal valet services.

Time will tell how these companies fare in the future but the point is about continuous evolution. Un-commoditizing strongly and actively is the driving factor. A decade ago, an inability to pinpoint your competition would have been most damaging to a business. But Amazon, Apple and Google have fully leveraged the scale of e-commerce and digital.

From our previous section, societal values change, niche becomes main-stream, and that's the biggest un-quantified threat – people shun what becomes too common. Or they find a way to balance out the commonplace with things that are different with new attributes that are emerging as the broader need has been satisfied.

- We needed a single, universal place to buy goods from in a cost effective and reliable manner. We needed a place to bring sellers together. Does this base platform now lead to a desire for something more local?

- We needed a universal search tool that could give us information on virtually anything. Does this base platform now lead to a desire for something more customized and tailored?

- Samsung came in with their Smart Phones because fans of the Apple iPhone were growing in number. That base was no longer a niche, which in itself was a big threat to the senses and aspirations of many people. The trend created a polarization and a natural tendency to adopt something different. Will other competitors identify and capitalize on other parts of this ecosystem?

The Dimensions of Un-Commoditization

In this section, let's now review the many dimensions of un-commoditization to drive home the fact that the possibilities are endless if we just persevere. Many of us don't even think about all items below to see how we are different.

Below are many possible dimensions of un-commoditization for us to consider. Remember, un-commoditization is not simply having a different product or price. It's about showing how we are different when all else remains constant. For example:

- How would Starbucks show they are different if another such specialty coffee shop opens in the neighborhood?

- How does Dell show they are different from HP when it comes to the same laptop computer?

Sometimes we may decide we don't need un-commoditization when we are one among the few in a chosen market. Those scenarios may arise, but forward looking plans help companies make the right decisions in the present so the doors to the future remain open, just in case. Perhaps the answer is in tailored services, perhaps in launching different brands. Whatever the case, constantly building on the points of un-commoditization with an eye on the future will allow us to make the right decisions when the time comes.

1. The Mundane Un-Commoditization Factors

These are the basics when we have nothing more to offer except claims. Most of these are easily copied and are temporary. When the customer asks "why should I choose you over another," if all we have are mushy things to say like "we care about you" or "we place our customers' needs first," we need to think again. Unless we can pinpoint those specific things that matter to our customers and make us different, these don't go far towards making an impact.

All other things remaining more or less equal - such as price and customer segments, these commodity factors of un-commoditization include claims such as:

☐ Better quality
☐ Better vision
☐ Better customer service
☐ Better affinity

We can never win a war based on the above claims if these don't reflect in the DNA of what we do. Without a top down focus on clearly outlining the differences, and driving bottoms-up culture and practices to excel at those very aspects – perhaps while even ignoring the other distractions – the journey of un-commoditization is a futile one. All it takes is a great deal of marketing investment while creating absolutely no difference.

• Consider the many upstarts coming up to provide pre-packed, pre-measured ingredients and recipes for home cooking. This was a new market opportunity that has now been tapped. But as we cycle through the web, it's hard to really pinpoint how each is different. What barriers are they building?

• Consider banks, cellular service provider companies, cable companies, insurance firms - the list goes on and on. Unless these companies are willing to concede on certain attributes, they will be forever fighting the price and customer-churn war. Yes, they have two-year contracts and higher switching costs but is that a factor on which to bet the future?

Contrast that with how Target was able to successfully create a little bit of a difference from Wal-Mart, or how Ford is beginning to distance itself from the other US car makers when it comes to quality and engineering. It takes years for these to start showing effect. The Target REDcard is a tool that sets up Target for great innovation.

Un-commoditization may initially seem to be cost a little more, but it really doesn't if it is transformational. It results in a fuller, more balanced value proposition that saves many other hidden costs we may not even be looking at today. These costs are spread across our value chain right from creating customer awareness, customer acquisition, to customer service and retention. In the modern connected world, we just have to be different and be able to reinforce it. It's uncomfortable to question traditional wisdom and practices that have worked forever, but we must venture, and experiment, or we'll be fighting for survival. Banks, cable companies, insurance, retail – you name it - and all of them are seeing their business models in massive turmoil. Then why not also transform the way we engage with customers? The time is now.

2. Process-based Un-Commoditization Factors

Process-based factors go towards qualifying our mundane differentiators. If done well, these can serve to extend the life of our everyday differentiators, and result in a long term and favorable customer perception.

☐ Who we serve
☐ What we won't offer
☐ Our procurement processes
☐ Our technology and interoperability
☐ Our sales and finance models
☐ Our supply chain processes
☐ Our transaction and commerce methodology
☐ Our customer service philosophy

These factors take us one step closer to creating a transformational un-commoditization package. However, more often than not, these become internally focused if the purpose of the business is forgotten in the race for growth. Examples:

- For a while, the auto insurance companies were able to differentiate using their claims handling processes. By innovating in how fast they handled new reports, and how comfortable they made customers feel, they were able to play right into the sentiments of the customers. As that advantage fades away, they are once again in a cycle that begs for "what's different?" As the online model evolves, auto insurance is again coming down to price comparison at the end of every term. Advanced data analytics and targeting will save the day for the short term as they are able to treat customers in a differentiated way based on a prediction of how they drive and what they care for most. And that analytics will probably open doors to better customer engagement. In the end, the online world is not faceless. We may not see the transaction, but there's still a human at the other end, with real sentiments and real needs.

- Think of Starbucks again. Their claimed process of picking and delivering the best beans has given them the positioning of better coffee along with their process of serving it in a great environment. There is no other easy option for premium coffee but as niche coffee houses are cropping up, they have had to diversify in other areas to continue to maintain the novelty. Their position at the emotional end of the customer interaction spectrum will probably be unchallenged for a while. But they must continue to find new ways of showcasing their differences in terms of how consumers are benefitted at the physical end of the customer interaction spectrum.

- Wal-Mart differentiated on price and better value because of its supply chain and procurement processes. But as online came to be, and customer experience became primary, those benefits may be beginning to fade. While Wal-Mart continues to have a large following, they need to try alternate approaches to improve the overall basket at check out. An example of that is apparel.

- Amazon differentiated because of its supply chain, seller market place and targeted cross-sell capabilities. The customer service provided peace of mind. Visiting Amazon is the default action for many buyers. As pricing advantages disappear, and focused online retail stores emerge, those initial advantages may be fleeting. Hence, Amazon is creating a more expansive ecosystem around digital to keep itself in the lead.

3. Culture-based Un-Commoditization Factors

These factors show passion and bring out the purpose behind the business. It takes a lot to sustain this differentiation beyond a few years because it is so tightly linked to the beliefs of the founders. But when this becomes a professional branded strategy, and when the services and products align to that strategy, these factors can truly provide the un-commoditization factors a business needs to survive the onslaught of price wars and popular brands.

- ☐ The purpose - Why the business was started
- ☐ Ethnic or cultural affiliation
- ☐ Our culture, our attitude
- ☐ Unique backgrounds and traits of our employees
- ☐ How we grew
- ☐ Why we won't be different in some ways
- ☐ Place of business
- ☐ Historical affiliation

These dimensions will build an identity-based linkage with customers.

Summary – The Principle of Un-Commoditization

From the types of un-commoditization we examined in this chapter, the one underlying rule that I want to leave us with is this:

"Our un-commoditization must lead to a visible difference to our customers. Otherwise, it's time to go back to the drawing board."

Choosing the right un-commoditization for our products or services is critical. And emotional differentiators are almost always a must to create for every firm. Whether these differentiators are about belonging, affluence, safety or peace of mind, they will become ingrained in the minds of our customers, leading to lasting results and providing a cushion in scenarios when the product line itself is under siege by new or existing competitors. A life without un-commoditization is about price and chance.

In the end, for any un-commoditization strategy to be durable, it must be driven from the alignment of organizational culture to the un-commoditization factors. All too often, culture is spoken of in isolation, without a real link to the business processes of the company. The next time we see those posters on the walls, and the rewards and recognition program we have established, it's time to ask "How are we leveraging and linking these slogans to the customer touch-points and in our core products and services?"

4

The Principle of Presenting

The Principle of Presenting provides the framework for an organization to adhere to its purpose, stitching together a product portfolio in a way that in its entirety, logically meets the customer's needs.

"It is not from the benevolence of the butcher, the brewer, or the baker, that we expect our dinner, but from their regard to their own interest. We address ourselves, not to their humanity but to their self-love, and never talk to them of our own necessities but of their advantages."

– Adam Smith, Wealth of Nations

Adam Smith explains the classic "order in chaos" concept in his masterpiece. But in a connected world, modern organizations need a little more stewardship to survive.

The Principle of Presenting is about presenting a company aligned to its mission statement and raison d'être, not as individual business units or products. The difference is stark. A mission statement is often broad and all encompassing, arising from recognition of a customer need that must be addressed. At founding, or even when a new business line is launched, the goals are lofty, focused on the customer, powered by the grit and determination of the founders and their vision, fueled by the passionate energy that accompanies the thrill of being at the helm of driving a new agenda. But after the organizational dynamics and business constraints have taken their toll, what can result is a fragmented firm chasing to meet fragmented financial targets. The result is often obsolescence or the position of an also ran struggling for share in a crowded market. It takes strong leadership and a very focused, market-aligned product set for a firm to stay relevant to its customers.

The Principle of Presenting provides the framework for an organization to adhere to its purpose, stitching together a product portfolio in a way that in its entirety, logically meets the customer's needs.

The Five Blind Men and the Elephant

There was once a village where five blind men lived. One morning there was excitement all around as people rushed to take a look and exclaimed "an elephant is coming!" The five blind men had never seen an elephant before and they were determined to find out what it looked like. In a busy marketplace, they walked up to the elephant and began to examine him.

The first blind man felt the legs and said "I know, the elephant seems like a set of massive pillars."

The second blind man felt the trunk and said "No it doesn't. Are you dreaming? It looks like a giant snake."

The third blind man felt the tail and said "You both are wrong. The elephant looks like a strong rope."

The fourth blind man touched the body and said "Nonsense, the elephant seems like a great big wall."

The fifth blind man was by the ears and said "What are you talking about, the elephant is like huge banana leaves."

And so the five blind men quarreled and fought. They were not right individually, but they were not completely wrong either. They just had incomplete views of what an elephant looked like.

The same is true of how we view our businesses and our customers. In fact, how our customers view us also follows the same pattern. And that's precisely the gap that the Principle of Presenting attempts to resolve.

The Concept behind the Principle of Presenting

When a firm sells an individual product, it is meeting a portion of the customer's needs. And over time, a firm advances into adjacent areas to slowly meet broader customer needs or to attract different types of customers.

- A razor manufacturer may make disposable razors and electric razors, and then begin to make shaving gels as well as after shaving lotions and products

- A bank begins to offer retirement planning services and wealth management services

- A software products company begins to make software in newer areas

And so on. Almost all businesses started out narrow and then expanded. Banks started by offering savings accounts. Amazon started as an online book seller. Google started as a search company. Microsoft started as an operating system. Many Indian software services companies started with economical and quality offshore IT project delivery. Unilever and P&G likely started with soap or cream. Nike probably started with shoes. In some cases, companies assume new identities as markets change and their original brand no longer covers their new line. 3M, KFC, LG are some examples of companies that overhauled their identities.

How we advance and evolve as a firm is predicated on many different factors such as competitive pressures, opportunities, and vision. But what is common is that businesses expand and launch new products and offerings.

The foundation of The Principle of Presenting is that more often than not, the product line extensions and expansions are linked by a common thread. That thread is around a broader, underlying customer need and the organization's purpose. The Principle of Presenting is about tying the various products and services together in a way that meets the underlying customer need and facilitates seamless interaction. It is about minimizing the gap between the combined value proposition of all our product offerings —our entire product portfolio - and the customer's need.

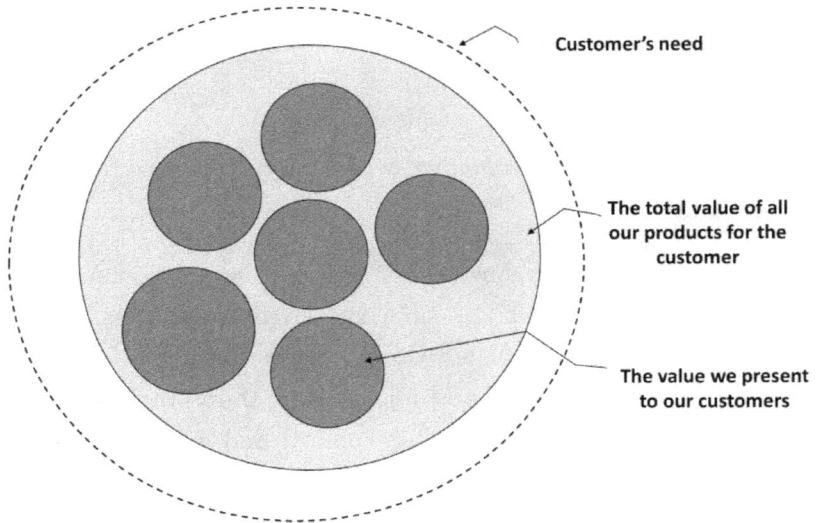

Figure 21: The gaps in our value proposition

If our business looks and behaves with a single minded focus on the customer, then we've got it mastered. But if it operates in silos, and makes the customer jump through hoops to understand and buy our products, then we have a problem.

We need to ask:

When a customer thinks about us, do they think of the many

different needs they have that can be met by the many products we have? Or can they automatically, instinctively state their need in a way that ALL of our products can collectively meet?

The difference is important. For example,

- Everyone may know that banks offer multiple products that can meet many different financial needs. But we can also probably guess the amount of budgets allocated to cross-sell and upsell.

- A local supermarket may offer loyalty, shipping, online ordering, online recipes, email coupons, ingredient checks, allergy advice and many other convenience features to the customer. Think of your supermarket. I bet that only a miniscule proportion of customers will know and use these features.

- A software product or services firm may offer to satisfy multiple aspects of a client's requirements, but are those products and services being presented as whole, aligned with the client's business-technology strategy? Or are they being brought to the table when the client asks for it, or when an opportunity is identified?

The costs of not adhering to The Principle of Presenting can be seen by simply observing the multitude of advertising and awareness programs underway at most firms. When these programs are integrated with a seamless customer experience, then the gap between value and need is smallest. However, when these programs are add-ons to the original value proposition offered, then we are simply not positioned to meet our customers' needs. We are operating as multiple independent companies who offer these products.

In fact, the scenario is akin to a marketplace. We show case all our products, we extoll the virtues of them at different stalls, and leave the selection, evaluation and buying of products to customers. This scenario is acceptable for a marketplace with multiple vendors, but does not work well for the products and offerings of a single firm. Every time our firm is presented in this fashion to our customers, we fall further behind in the long term competitive race. And this phenomenon also opens up the doors for competition to jump in and chip away at our share.

The importance of The Principle of Presenting cannot be overemphasized. Consider the examples all around us. From the bank that sells credit cards and struggles to sell a savings account, to the services firm that struggles to penetrate further into different client portfolios. Even your favorite razor struggles to sell you diapers for your kids. All of these firms are probably looking at their customers from the vantage point of their own offerings and brands, thoroughly researching, targeting and positioning using many effective techniques. The only technique we don't use is to look at ourselves and imagine how a customer would perceive us and then annihilate our antiquated organizational structures to align with that single most important point of view. Organizational theory teaches us management, accountability, strategy, execution, control, but it hasn't evolved to show us how to align with the customer. We are all about brands, profit centers, service areas, regions and support functions. And then we get lost in the muddle and start treating these various entities as independent companies, opening the door to a new entrant to pull the rug from under our feet, or drag us down into the murky depths of competing on price.

Our Disconnect with the Customer

To put this principle into practice, let's borrow from The Principle of External Reinforcement. Customers and consumers are looking for much more than information about our products. They are looking to define their need, compare options and determine what is right for them. In order to do that, they must analyze how a product or service will fit in with the other products and services they are considering. Finally they will investigate how the new products or services will work with what they already have. All along, the supporting factors like price, variants and shipment will be considered.

The Principle of Presenting starts by thinking about this customer thought process. We must start with the customer, not the product. Think about how our products are positioned to customers today.

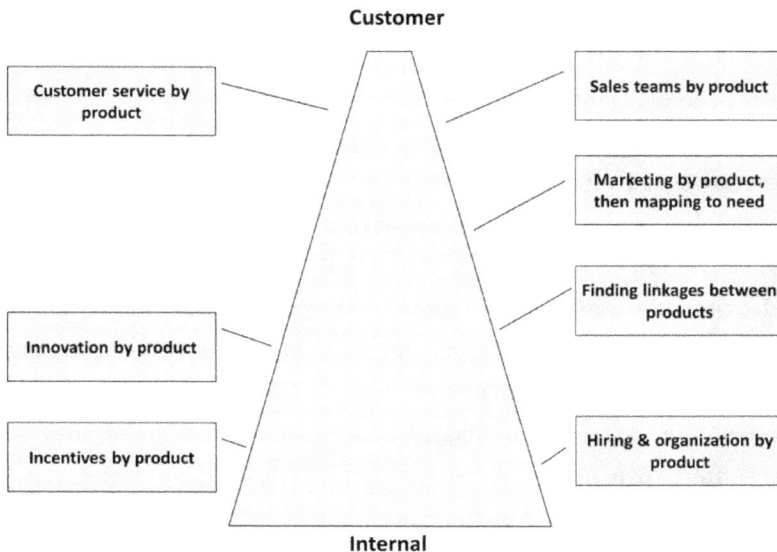

Figure 22: The way we go to the customer today

The gaps are obvious. There is a big disconnect between what we are designing and communicating, and what the customers are capable of hearing or are being told. The customer experience should revolve around the purpose of the products portfolio, and not a product itself. That is the significant difference from the current model. As the illustration on the next page indicates, we approach customers with individual products, failing to connect the dots with their overall needs. Our incentives are aligned by product, our organization is by product, our innovation is by product and it reflects in how we sell and market. In such a model, we have to create and rely on cross-functional programs to help bridge the gaps, and expect them to overcome the strongest barriers of all – motivating people. Why would someone support these programs when their incentives are aligned by their own product? As a result progress reports are published, metrics are adjusted to reflect positive sentiments and everyone goes home happy – without really making a dent.

As we walk away after opening a bank account in the town we just moved to, the associate at the branch should not be saying "is there anything else I can help you with?" Instead she should be saying "nice meeting you and as discussed we'll meet next week to discuss your portfolio and see how you might want to optimize your investments." This result is only possible if the conversation revolved around the customer, not the savings account. When the conversation revolves around the customer, we focus on the purpose, and then tie our products together to meet that need. Regardless of our underlying strategy and vision, how the products and services are presented to a customer is paramount. And if we don't stitch those products together for the customer to make sense of them, someone else will.

More importantly, the messages delivered to customers will dictate how our organizations functions internally. If the output is in silos, the internal workings will be, too. To understand this, we only need to look at our own organizations. Chances are that our firms are organized by product line, and by geography. In my view, that model is not aligned with today's global digital economy, because it puts the onus of discovery on the customer, or worse still, the discovery never occurs because we focus on local customer relationships. Taking that relationship global is too complicated to achieve. The Principle of Presenting helps us think about creating exceptional customer engagement through a unified presentation to the customer.

- Multi-national companies are seeing their customers go global. As the pressure to improve the returns on operational investments increase, the trend of shared services is catching on. In addition, transformation agendas – like the one presented through the five principles – are being pursued or at least being seriously considered. In this scenario, B2B services providers selling multiple service and product lines need an underlying common thread.

- Financial services institutions have looked to independent product and service providers to bridge the product portfolio gaps - travel insurance, international money cards, payment models, shopping loyalty programs, warranties etc. In addition, customers are beginning to interact globally. How can the underlying purpose be more strongly met?

These problems will seem insurmountable if examined through the traditional lens that looks inside out at the problem – what services and products do we provide today, and how should we connect them or make them universal? That's a complicated question to answer. It's easier to comprehend if we reverse the lens – what do our customers need and how do we cater to that? What's worse is that in a firm focused on products and geographies, we may not even be asking this question.

The digital economy has bridged many isolated communication channels. Customers have access to peer networks, independent sources of information and credible, voluntary advice from experts. In a connected economy, customers don't have to do more than fire up their Internet browser and type in "reviews of <their product>" to get many different perspectives from people of all walks of life. Not every comment will be useful, accurate or objective, but it's enough to make customers reconsider their initial choices and motivations. Just like in the case of The Principle of External Reinforcement, if our products are not presented so they help each other with a singular focus on customer needs, our engagement with customers will be subpar.

The Relationship Context of our Channels

Consider any channel – direct sales, direct online, reseller, partner and others – the core performance of the channels is based on basic criteria such as share of total sales, growth in percentage share, and cost of sales made.

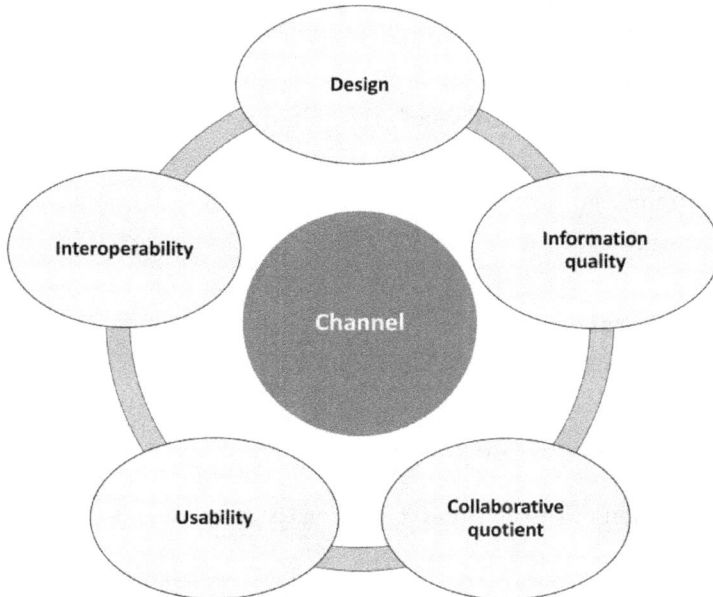

Figure 23: Basic construct of a channel

In the digital age, there is tremendous focus on improving the effectiveness of channels by streamlining processes, making the right information available in real time, and reducing the inherent costs of executing through the channel. We look at aspects such as:

- **Interoperability** of the channel which means how it works with other channels to present a seamless experience to the customer. This is also being termed as multi-channel, and being measured as Omni-Channel effectiveness from a customer perspective.

- **Design** of the channel which includes the processes, governance, reporting etc.

- **Usability** of the channel which includes user experience, mobile and online capabilities to look for information and engage in various transactions – commercial or otherwise.

- **Information quality** of the channel which is largely the supporting product information such as brochures, client testimonials, data about the customer, specifications, and other material.

- **Collaborative quotient** of the channel which includes how people work together to meet their goals. The collaboration may be between different organizations, or between various internal groups which work together.

As illustration of the channel, consider these scenarios:

- For a B2B products company selling complex configurable products, the partner channel is an important contributor to success. Partners may identify opportunities, and work with the product sales teams as they work to close the contracts with customers. Sales cycles are long and opportunities are generally tracked through a CRM (Customer Relationship Management) system, and also through various online and offline mechanisms, which often include the customer.

- A consumer product is sold and distributed across a region or nationally through salespeople working with distributors who in turn work with the product manufacturer and who in turn feeds the channel with promotions and inventory based on forecasts.

- For a retailer, engaging and interacting with customers over online, social and physical store channels is critical today. And data from previous transactions and from interactions over multiple channels is analyzed to define the next best action for the retailer in their interaction with the customer.

- A direct channel such as the e-commerce channel allows companies to engage and sell directly to customers without additional middlemen. These are most notably retailers, insurance companies, banks, software as a service companies and media companies among many others. Many traditional firms are also introducing direct channels in addition to their distributor channels. Growth of the direct e-Commerce channels means a reduction in operational costs, establishment of direct customer relationships and typically an increase in margins.

Today, these channels are largely based on products, not the customers. They've all been designed from the perspective of pushing products through, not from the perspective of meeting customer needs.

And as new entrants and incumbents aggressively un-commoditize themselves by positioning their products from a customer's vantage point, the upgrade of the channel is probably the most transformational trend we will see ripping through the marketplace in the coming years.

That brings us to the relationship context of a channel. The Principle of Presenting is all about the relationship, or a customer, and then percolates down to the product to align it correctly according to the customer need.

The Principle of Presenting brings up the following new dimensions of the channel:

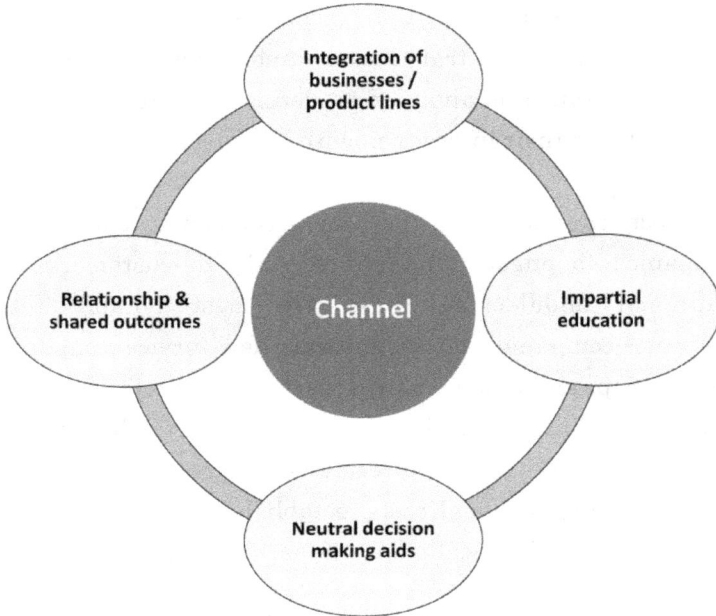

Figure 24: Emerging dimensions of the channel

- **Integration of businesses / products lines** - the channel is not about products, but about customer needs, and how the products collectively come together to meet a customer need.

- **Impartial education** - the information quality on the channel is defined by educating and guiding the customers about where they are, how they should look at their problems and how they could embark on a journey to meet their needs. That's a shift from product brochures and specifications availability.

- **Consultative, collaborative** tools and calculators that customers can use themselves, or which the channel participants can use to help the customers. All users including customers may interact through these tools and go through the exploration together.

- **Relationships** instead of historical information about product sales and trends, implying that the channel now begins to be the driver of consultative selling, sharing the responsibility for the outcomes instead of pushing the burden of the decision on the customer because they have to deal with the decision they end up making.

Let's see how these additional dimensions will manifest themselves, and how the channel re-orientation will help.

- B2B product companies would align their channels as per customer needs rather than product segments, and jointly with partners, would take the customers through a process of discovery and goal setting. The goal of engaging the customers is to discover and meet their needs, thus placing an emphasis on the total solution, rather than only trying to identify areas where a product can be fitted. This will enhance all the existing channel metrics as well. The biggest change is that various products will come together for consideration as the discovery starts from the customer need or pain point.

- Retailers will not only push products based on customer interaction, but also tie in the context of the customer's interaction. They'll ask the question, "Why is the customer looking for this?" and then subsequently move to "What could help the customer meet that need?" Consumers looking at yogurt in the grocery store would be given choices based on whether they are on a diet plan or holding a party. Of course, it's not always possible to have this interaction when a customer is in the grocery aisle. Instead, the purchase cycle starts long before that moment of truth. Complementing this with The Principles of Customer Interaction and External Reinforcement ensures being an aide throughout the customer decision cycle. In the next chapter we'll also identify how to use the powerful Principle of Completion. My view is that triggering a self -fueling process cultivates strong customer relationships highly resistant to competition.

- Consumer product firms will now work with the distributors and field sales teams to build a map of the customers (e.g. retailers), based on consumer trends, and help the retailers improve their overall basket instead of every sales person pushing their individual product category to the retailers' shelves. The focus will be on retailer ROI not product sales, because the latter would take care of itself as a consequence. Ignoring retailer ROI would be akin to an ostrich burying its head in the sand, simply waiting for a predator to come and get it.

- E-Commerce providers will evolve from being an online menu driven catalog of departments and inventory to be customer persona driven where possible. Imagine that an online retailer recommends products based on how well they fit with you, and presents them thematically in addition to displaying what other customers have also bought. The website for banks, and their branches and ATMs, would be based on who you are and what you already have.

To successfully make inroads the model has to be inverted like this:

Customer

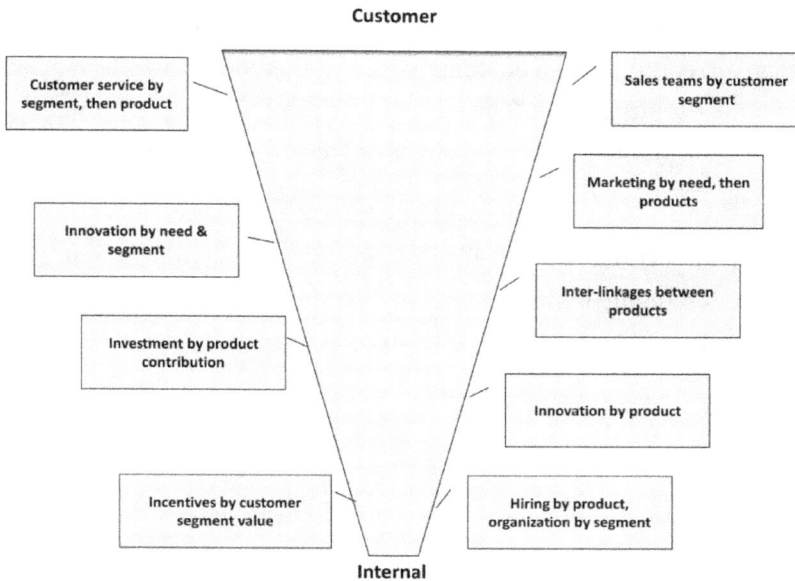

Customer service by segment, then product

Innovation by need & segment

Investment by product contribution

Incentives by customer segment value

Sales teams by customer segment

Marketing by need, then products

Inter-linkages between products

Innovation by product

Hiring by product, organization by segment

Internal

Figure 25: The path to the customer as per The Principle of Presenting

Here, the product is no longer the guiding unit of measurement when it comes to customer engagement in the digital age. Even though a product (or brand) from our portfolio may have the largest share of customers, The Principle of Presenting is not satisfied by silo approaches. And that implies that significant value remains unclaimed on the table. It means that as a firm, we are trying to break into the minds of the customers through expensive, traditional techniques when we already have a trusted place in the customers' mind through other products. The new way is to focus on being a partner to the customer, not a seller. It may seem counterintuitive but if we only think about our own journey as a customer, we'll see why this method will fast become the bulwark of customer engagement.

The new model illustrates the power of The Principle of Presenting. How we integrate business and product lines, align them to our raison d'être and engage customers in a dialog in our own living room makes all the difference. The purpose of the business is brought out in this new model, and it's obvious that the purpose transcends products.

In the next section, we will discuss best practices to overcome some common challenges in order to implement The Principle of Presenting.

Key challenges While Implementing The Principle of Presenting

It's a daunting task to be able to execute well on The Principle of Presenting. There are several important questions to ask:

1. How do we keep brands separate in the eyes of the customer?

Keeping some kinds of products separate in the eyes of the customer is important. And the requirement varies by type of industry. If you remember the Customer Interaction Index, companies where the customer interaction index is low are more likely to try and keep brands separate. They would prefer the brand engagement to be supreme because they operate on the emotional end of the spectrum. Consumer goods manufacturers such as Proctor & Gamble might want to keep Pampers and Tide separate. The same goes for other consumer-oriented businesses like McDonalds or Chipotle. In some cases we need to reinforce consumer confidence by leveraging the strength of the umbrella brand such as Unilever, SC Johnson and P&G. In other cases separation is key to promote customer choice as in the case of McDonald's or Chipotle. There are of course many other successful strategies being followed by Nivea, Virgin, Shell etc.

While there are many different best practices for umbrella brands and varying degrees to which they are implemented, companies may need to scrutinize inter-brand links before launching initiatives to implement The Principle of Presenting. The underlying goal is meeting customer needs. If multiple products within a company together can better meet the customer need, increase the share of wallet in the company's favor and can address competitive advances, then The Principle of Presenting makes sense. The next chapter outlines how we can build a chain of links using The Principle of Completion. That is also a powerful way for brands to work together.

On the other hand, some types of organizations would want to explicitly cross-sell products. In most cases, these companies have an inherently high Customer Interaction Index. Their potential for tackling the physical customer engagement end of the spectrum is much higher. They also enjoy the benefits of a strong emotional connection with its customers. Banks, insurance firms, software product firms, consulting and services firms, retailers, and many others would want to implement The Principle of Presenting to its fullest.

2. How do we avoid overloading the customer with information?

In the digital age, customers are flooded with information; from us, our competitors, from advisors, from consultants and many independent experts. It only takes a second to Google our product or service and we will find all kinds of material such as:

- Customer reviews –positive and negative
- Ranking sites – how our product stacks up on many different dimensions
- Corporate news
- Brand fan pages
- Customer experiences
- Competitive comparisons
- Political linkages
- Reseller sites
- Expert communities
- Self-organized customer communities
- News associated with human rights
- Personal perceptions of what our brand is all about
- Advice on what our product or service should actually be doing

Add to the above our own initiatives:

- The promotions that we, our competitors and our channel (resellers, retailers, partners etc.) are running

- The advertisements – tackling the emotional end of the spectrum – that everyone is running

It seems incredibly complex once we begin to map out a customer's decision making process with regards to our brands. For customers, that's not a problem at all. They pick up what appeals to them and what they've been convinced of both actively and passively. Or they just delay their decision while they do their research, or even trust someone's advice and take a chance.

The more businesses proceed from the vantage point of a customer's need and its context, the easier fulfilling that need becomes. A decision is made in our favor because over time customers have been conditioned on some beliefs. With these beliefs as a reference point, the final decision on our products is made. These beliefs range from emotional to the physical end of the spectrum. Some common implicit conditioning factors are tradition, safety, future readiness, reliability, familiarity, prestige, nostalgia etc. The Principle of Presenting can help with either augmenting, or breaking the conditioning of the mind by following a different path from the traditional. And if one customer action reinforces another previous decision by supporting the context of the decision through The Principle of Presenting, we enable the customer to take a decision with the confidence that their entire needs spectrum is being satisfied.

3.   How do we meet customers where they like to be?

Where do we go to meet our customers in the digital age? Is our own website even relevant? Super Bowl advertisements are expensive, short lived and not for everyone. So, we try to be everywhere hoping to engage our customers – Facebook, Twitter, Pinterest, and so on. We treat each of these avenues as a traditional channel, running promotions and gimmicks while measuring success by way of people engaging with our messages, or becoming a Facebook fan or a Twitter follower. We also run product communities hoping to get user engaged. Then we treat the community as a channel and push coupons and promotions to it, hoping folks will get hooked and better engaged.

There's nothing wrong with trying to use a medium as a channel and measuring it separately. The point I'm trying to make is the channel must be leveraged and brought in sync with The Principle of Presenting. Every time The Principle of Presenting is not followed, it leaves something untapped and underutilized in terms of customer engagement, revenues, affinity, organizational culture, competitiveness and even cost savings.

What are we going to do to maximize the untapped potential presented by The Principle of Presenting? If we really want to take the radical view, we could only measure ourselves in terms of customer segment who buys a set of products or brands, instead of measuring our success by sales of products or brands. But that would challenge a lot of traditional practices and require significant investments to overhaul the information systems. Plus, humans would oppose it, too.

Rather, we can make incremental progress towards that goal. At the beginning, we may just want to make the customer engagement seamless. We no longer want customers to have to figure out how a company's various products play with each other and work for them. They know it's important, but they'd appreciate if we would do it for them instead of making sales pitches and creating promotions. Promotions and sales notifications are important, but we should provide customers with a reference point to evaluate the applicability of the sales tactics. What could these reference points be?

- For consumer-oriented businesses, the immediate reference points could be peer pressure, looking up to someone, seeing an advertisement, aspiring to a personal goal, wanting to try it out, being part of a community etc.

- For a business customer, the reference points are a core need, being forward looking and aligning to the vision of contributing to success. Customers want to make a decision to buy a product or service that fits that need and aligns with their professional goals, explicit and implicit.

For both of these, The Principle of Presenting highlights the premise that information needs to be made accessible in ways that appeal to the customer, making it effortless for customers to consume and comprehend it. Customers like to know whether the products are even applicable to them. And if yes, how exactly will they benefit. They'd like to be advised rather than be sold the biggest possible deal.

As customers:

- We'd appreciate tools that don't sell, but help.

- We'd like the seller to understand and sell us in the context of what we already do, or have done with them. Otherwise, we have to go back and research this on our own, anyway.

And as businesses:

- We'd like to address the customers overall need or a set of related needs because our products portfolio evolved with that vision.

- We'd like to ensure that customers get the best possible bargain for their particular situation, and buy more of the products from us.

From The Principle of External Reinforcement, we know that the reason behind the new way to engage customers is obvious. We trust and connect with channels that lead us to the "right" decision. Channels that successfully accomplish this become our go-to partners. And in this social world, that positioning also results in customers themselves becoming a contributor to that advice. We love to receive, and we also love to help. It's just human nature.

The Principle of Presenting builds on that model by bringing all products together in an intuitive way for customers. Consider these following simple industry scenarios that support this model of "Purpose driven purchase".

Consumer Banking

There's a reason that when we have to get a new credit card or an account, we look to third party sites and opinion to give us feedback. If banks focus on educating us on what fits us best, and given the fact that the products vary somewhat in features, my guess is that the first bank to do this will win big. Customers need a reference point to validate their choices and feel good about the choices they make; more so when they already have a product from the bank. Such a positioning will then lead to a business case towards customizable products which can overcome the mass marketing hurdles banks face today.

This implies that the traditional model of product-based presentation is inadequate. After the recent financial crisis, the trend of simple banking really took hold. Customers are more aware of their costs of banking, and more conscious of taking matters in their own hands. The two mutually offsetting trends are:

1. The population of digital and business savvy customers is increasing. This is attributed to better access to the Internet and the ability to collaborate and share. Advice, experiences and feedback are available at the touch a button and the barriers to information have been reduced. People know more about more products, and are more aware of their financial goals and best practices to reach them.

2. At the same time, the pace of life has dramatically increased. People are doing more things at the same time than ever before. The availability of information is not just an access issue, it's an attention issue. Consequently, the proportion of really business savvy consumers is not likely to grow as fast or as comprehensively as we think.

The end result is that customers are creating new simplistic rules about what they expect. They know they have to start early towards retirement, they know they should bargain for more loyalty rewards, and push for fewer fees on the services to which they subscribe.

Think of the concept of "banking made simple". The most talked about banks are those that are able to make banking available and user friendly. We are moving towards a future where the presentation will focus on the consumer, not on the products. Websites and calculators that are presently organized by products will have to give way to a presentation by a customer persona – either anonymous or individual based.

The creation of self-selection tools by several banks was a step in that direction. The tools ask the customer about who they are – are they students, are they small business owners, do they travel etc. The customers were then given additional choices and presented with the credit cards that were best suited to their lifestyles. Now we need to move beyond products and features. In the past we linked to the immediate goals, but failed to provide a deeper connection to the customer's identity. What resulted are elaborate programs to get customers to make their first transaction quickly. Even as the number of customers increased, the amount of unused credit available to customers posed another challenge for banks for financial risk management. Programs were then initiated to close or reduce these credit lines.

Following The Principle of Presenting also ensures that the focus is on improving the products per customer, rather than on tackling individual business unit metrics. Problems with incentives are compounded when products themselves seem to compete with each other, e.g. debit and credit cards by the same bank.

What we need in the future are customer-centric processes that align to The Principle of Presenting. Imagine what would have happened if the customer was guided through a process of self-discovery. Instead of having to click on a menu that says "credit cards" or an offer of "0% balance transfer for 3 months," the customers were brought into the system through a discovery process of their financial goals, with the entire product portfolio coming together to aid this discovery. By mandating this journey, customer engagement would make a complete about turn. Instead of being apprehensive, the customer is engaged, and the bank finally knows how to optimize the use of its website. In fact, the next chapter on The Principle of Completion will provide further insights on how to implement this model of customer centric discovery.

The Retail Dilemma

Sending customers coupons and promotions is great, but it's only half the job done. How about if retailers help customers decide what they should buy and what they should avoid– even if they don't sell what customers really need? By entering into a partnership with the customer, it's likely they would cut down dramatically on costs, and by knowing what customers want (and their shopping baskets), they may also be able to transform their inventory management.

The retailer's dilemma boils down to this: do we know the purpose of customers when they are picking items off the shelves, or adding items to their online shopping carts?

In most cases, we don't. We try to get through the cross-sell process by showing offers to customers based on analytics of historical data, and hoping that the offer would stick.

- Online retail stores display other items that the customer could consider. This display is based on what other customers also bought. Close, but not a guaranteed match. A deduction is better than nothing however, and this mechanism has increased in popularity in the past several years since Amazon first used it. But in today's times when online inventory has increased significantly, and when purchases are more frequent, across more outlets and hence more unrelated, we need to find better ways to make this correlation.

- Retailers – both online and offline – are still organized by product and category aisles. It's what we are used to. But as we saw in the case of pre-made dinners, consumers would sacrifice a lot for convenience and simplicity. And what better way than goal oriented shopping? What's the menu or diet plan on their minds? For which occasion are customers buying dresses? These are questions retailers need to answer to really make a dent in customer engagement. It's just like the banking scenario. Everything else is just window dressing.

What can help us build context? Recently, there are many new innovations that have come into practice. They provide incentives to customers for sharing their purchase habits and history – create grocery lists, scan purchase receipts, enter the items on to a wish-list, let sites know when specific coupons were redeemed etc. These are steps in the right direction. What is needed is a way to tie all of this information together into The Principle of Presenting instead of just feeding it into more traditional campaigns and promotions. The grocery delivery sector especially has great potential because over time it can predict and auto-populate a shopping list. But unless combined with the real activities customers are carrying out – e.g. weekly recipes and real time feedback - this will again become a game of analytics and guesswork.

The Principle of Presenting can bring all these elements together by focusing on building the customer persona and organizing everything around that. Retailers especially will benefit greatly as this context is built up through the five principles. Not only can retailers engage customers, but they can actually know, not only predict what the customers are looking for. That knowledge will dramatically improve operational costs on the one hand, while triggering the positive cycle of engaging customers on an individual basis.

Professional Services

Some of the primary criteria customers look for in professional services is credibility - familiarity, expertise, experience, past results – and price. The situation may be reversed in some cases but that's either a first timer mistake or a learning process, not an accepted practice to base our business on. The Principle of Presenting focuses on improving credibility in the customer's eyes and better educating them with respect to their needs. Marketing may get us through the door, but it doesn't make the sale, at least in a consistent manner.

Helping customers meet other customers, and sharing best practices and means to achieve their goals are more likely to bring in the customer.

Chances are that a professional services firm or sole proprietorship engages in multiple services. Actually, for better background setting, let's call these services as "ways to help the customer." That's because the same service may help the customer in multiple ways.

- An information technology services firm will probably provide the same type of skills to solve many different business situations.

- An electrician or plumber will be helping the customer with many different needs, some of them even life threatening.

- A logistics provider will carry goods for numerous businesses, all with their own specific quirks.

The Principle of Presenting for professional services comes down to being consultative. How do we take our entire basket of services, and present it in a way that draws customers in with an expectation of learning a little more about managing the problem they have, or one they will surely have soon.? It's about prevention as well as the cure.

The consultative approach opens the doors to problems or symptoms that the customer doesn't even know exists. It orients our entire basket of services to discovering the unexpressed customer need and providing ways to meet it.

For example, in this age of the technology driven digital revolution, everyone is talking about multi-channel commerce and contextual customer engagement. The problem of multi-channel commerce is not just about the customer experience channels such as mobile or web. It's way beyond the latest e-Commerce platform or the best mobile application. The need for a seamless multi-channel experience can only be met effectively if the entire technology stack is aligned to that need. That includes databases, analytics, middleware that connects applications, business process management software and all the other plumbing that is needed. Any firm that presents a single capability to the customer is doing itself and the customer a significant disservice. Unless you thrive on commoditized services where customers have a couple of parameters and a price tag associated with them, it pays to think of the big picture.

The Metrics of People

The essence of an organization is its people. As organizations get larger and more complex, they need a way to hold people accountable to performance. The easiest way to judge performance is metrics.

As Adam Smith outlined in his classic masterpiece, when individuals take care of their own goals, they often serve the larger good. But the principle is a general one and applicable at the macro level. There are salient examples of waste all around us as we serve our own interests without regard for the environment. The same is true for an organization. In fact we have various goals such as financial, customer satisfaction and competitive goals. And each of these goals is monitored by the inside-out perspective of products and services. While we may be meeting the immediate objectives, the business world is transforming into a race where the agile and the connected are winning. There is a dire need to turn this model to be outside-in. The Principle of Presenting is critical in this new economy. Figures 22 and 25 have presented this concept visually.

The Principle of Presenting is tough to follow because we often measure and hold people accountable to incomplete metrics. It's not deliberate, but it just happens as a natural course of evolution. There's no one tasked with keeping the original fabric together. What ultimately results is that different people clamor to meet different and often conflicting metrics, vying for a greater share of the available and common organizational resources. They become like the five blind men - not looking at the customer, but thinking of and aspiring to meet just one dimension of how a specific customer can help them achieve their personal goals, not that of the organization.

To implement the Principle of Presenting, we must refer to the market research we performed when we thought about making each individual product or creating a service. The business case was predicated on several factors, and the most important sections we are looking for are about:

- Why that product is NOT a fit for the customer
- How it fits into the overall products strategy
- What are the overlaps between products

The Principle of Presenting is best achieved when we can still align to the focused value proposition behind the product or service creation. This is done by arranging our products and services as per the aspirations and needs of our customers.

Every customer will need multiple products to satisfy their needs. B2B strategists may arrange these as per the value chain, and further segregate by functions and roles within each part of the value chain. B2C firms may create a map based on frequency and time of usage, and then further segregate by personas or time of day. Then we create a map that outlines the links between the needs, products and services.

Summary – The Principle of Presenting

To determine that framework for our specific business, we must do seven things in preparation:

1. Draw an org chart, including all key groups and stakeholders.
2. Then erase that org chart.
3. Then on that blank paper, draw a symbolic picture of our customer
4. For each customer, create a journey according to their aspirations, interests and activities. For our customers who themselves have customers, we'll do this for their end customers, not our immediate customers.
5. Devise a few metrics around step # 4 to fully support or enhance the customer journeys.
6. Discard all reporting and analysis around all other metrics that determine someone's performance or bonus.
7. Define our organization to meet the new metrics.

The implications of this exercise are enormous and far reaching. Our entire approach will be realigned to the customer. By clarifying the performance metrics and measurement, the approach to The Principle of Presenting will not be open to interpretation anymore.

5

The Principle of Completion

Instead of analyzing actions and deriving correlations, we now analyze needs and create an appropriate experience based on the wholeness of our customers' identities. In short, we redefine customer centricity.

The Principle of Completion emphasizes that the spectrum of customer needs far exceeds what one organization can offer. Customer needs are not limited by an organization and its products. Consumers evaluate and buy products that meet various needs; these are often similar products from different companies. What this means is that we must move on from joint ventures and partnerships that serve to satisfy the narrow need that our product offerings were intended to serve. Instead, we must move to begin to treat our customers in light of their overall needs and aspirations.

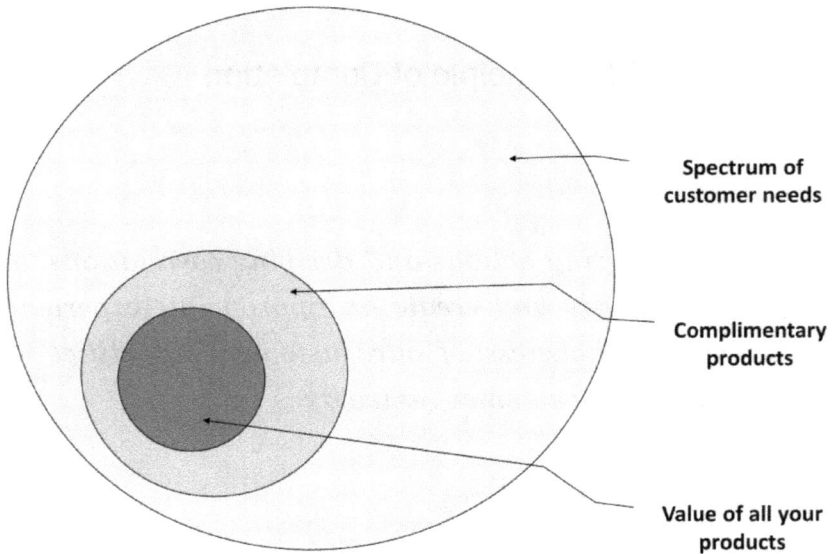

Figure 26: Our products and the entire spectrum of customer needs

The world today is connected, and in newer ways every day. This evolution requires businesses to collaborate and transform the definition of the channel to reach and engage with their customers. In the new digital age, the partnership models are set to undergo a dramatic transformation.

Traditionally, businesses have overcome the channel problem by making:

- Channel partners (for distribution)
- Field partners (for service)
- Outreach partners (for marketing)
- Technical partners (for manufacturing or R&D)
- And so on.

The intent has been to supplement our core capabilities where we need help. The focus has always been on partners that help us accomplish our core functions better, cheaper and faster. In essence we establish partnerships with the inside-out approach – looking at customers from our own vantage point.

The Principle of Completion suggests that going forward, ecosystems of companies will strongly drive the partnerships model. By ecosystems, I mean the wholeness of a customer's identity, not a specific need that our business seeks to satisfy. It follows that businesses that have nothing to do with the value chain of our own business will be strong candidates for partnerships.

These examples illustrate this point:

1. Where health and fitness centers had little connection to retail, they now often partner with health food manufacturers and retailers to develop joint programs to boost customer engagement and meet a need of the customer pursuing a healthy lifestyle. All three parties benefit by working together.

2. Where banks participate in the fitness and health arena by creating mechanisms for customers to pursue healthy habits in return for better banking benefits.

3. Where credit card companies that monitor spending and balances on their cards, would co-brand with not one, but multiple service providers and retailers to launch a multi-branded offering. All parties are now facilitators of customer needs based on overall spending patterns and wish lists.

These examples are just some predictions of what the future might hold, but they are not far from reality. A customer centric view implies that we must look at our organization outside-in through our customers' eyes.

1. When and where are they looking to fit in our product category?

2. What products are they fitting in and in which places that don't concern our products?

3. When they don't fit in with our product, what other products are they consuming?

The entire digital revolution that has laid traditional business obsolete is based on this principle. There is still a long way to go for the focus to shift to the customer needs. Today, we are still only taking advantage of the technology capabilities to upgrade existing business models. It's a significant jump, but only an incremental one when viewed from the vantage point of the Principle of Completion:

1. Amazon has expanded from being simply an online bookseller to a rapidly growing marketplace. It has adjusted its core service into the needs spectrum of the online world. It could have been satisfied by simply being an online store for books and music. But Amazon used its paid shipping model (Prime membership) and its marketplace to engage with changing customer behavior from music to movies to Kindle to everything under the sun. The focus

is still on Amazon though, not on the industry ecosystem.

2. Starbucks has effectively used its mobile application to accept payments from customers. Previously, Starbucks utilized a third party network, but with the new app its now driving more traffic, more engagement, more promotions and more loyalty. And if it expands its payment mechanisms to help other retailers, does Starbucks have a shot at being at the center of a shopping revolution?

3. Target has used its REDcard to reduce the cost of doing business while improving personalization and loyalty. The 5% discount is tough for most people to pass up. It remains to be seen how the REDcard will progress beyond Target to encompass the other networks that its customers leverage to meet their needs.

While interesting and often talked about, the successes so far are only the tip of the iceberg. The digital world offers such a huge potential, and most of it is still untapped.

Conglomerates with a Twist

For the past few decades, the conglomerate strategy – one holding company with many diverse and unrelated businesses – has been frowned upon. It was thought better to spin these businesses off as independent entities so they could create greater shareholder wealth and thrive on their own. The principle of completing oneself, doesn't reverse that, but brings that trend back 180 degrees, or halfway back.

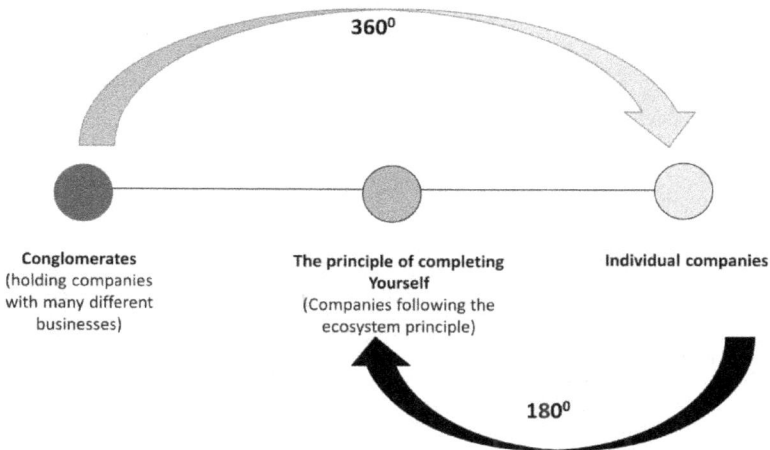

Figure 27: Conglomerates with a twist

Is this similar to being a supermarket? Wal-Mart had the vision of being a supermarket. It provided almost all ancillary services that one could imagine. Haircuts, prescription eye glasses, fast food, check cashing, credit cards, bank accounts and so on. If the concept of a supermarket is true, why was the vision only half successful? And isn't Amazon really just an online supermarket – an inventory and distribution partner to many businesses? Contrast that with Apple. Through its app store, has it created a conglomerate linked together by Apple phones and computers and an underlying payment ecosystem?

The Principle of Completion is much broader than spawning a conglomerate or creating platforms through which others can jump into your ecosystem. It's about anticipating industry disruptions and evolving to meet the linked and related needs of the customers. In short it's about bringing industry players together to collaborate on meeting customer needs.

The execution framework is:

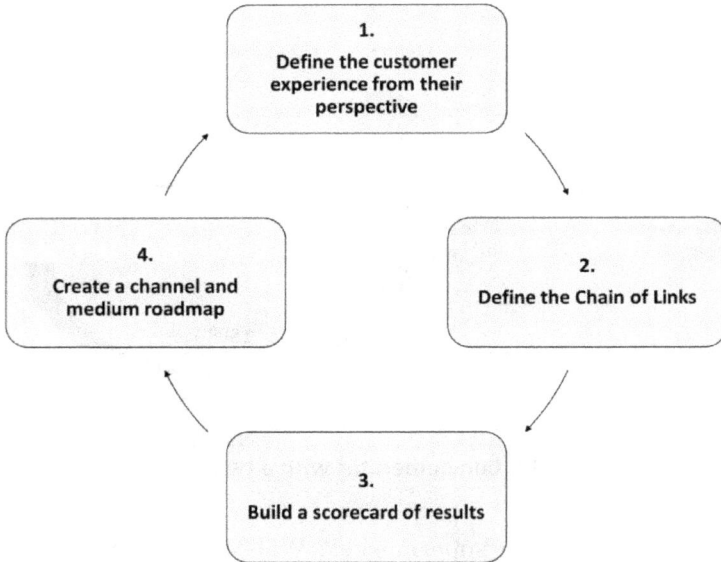

Figure 28: Execution framework for the Principle of Completion

Let's analyze each one individually.

1. Define the customer experience from their perspective, not ours

Customer choices are increasingly interlinked as boundaries between needs are falling. Even though the links may not be obvious, anticipating them and piloting initiatives will determine the true winner in the long term. There are examples all around us. Ever wonder how banks came up with credit cards, or how Amazon became a media powerhouse from being an online bookstore, or how mobile phones became central to Google's survival? The very concepts that companies applied before must continue to be applied. Only now in a connected world, we need to think in terms of ecosystems. To be successful in the digital world, we must ignore our product base when we traverse the customer needs and define the experience from their perspective.

Whereas these innovations came about through the ideas of innovative champions who could influence the vision of their companies, we now need a structured approach to make this the required thinking of modern day businesses.

When we examine customers (let's consider ourselves for consumer-oriented businesses), their needs extend far beyond a single company's products or services. We have traditionally tackled this with buyer personas. And then depending on how that persona buys our product, or how that persona learns about us, we attempt to inject ourselves in the conversation for consideration. The exercise is based on analysis of historical information, survey results, focus groups and just plain common sense.

Therefore, our approach so far has been to try to be noticed by the customer in the right places. We focus on creating interruptions which they may take note of. We send them an email, show them a promotion or price discount, entice them with a free trial, lead with expert advice about our product category or give them a coupon to encourage a future transaction. In all of these methods, what is common is a conversion statistic – we try, and we pray that a certain percentage will convert. And our entire life's mission is to improve that conversion percentage. I call this the *blind approach*.

Examples of the blind approach are:

- Online retailers show us products that we may like based on what we browsed before or based on items in our cart. They have a likelihood of purchase which is statistical in nature.

- Retailers and professional services firms send coupons every few weeks either based on past analysis or just randomly. Do they know when or what the consumer is going to purchase? Through continuous campaign uplift analysis they can probably predict that the percentage of people responding to promotions is going to be higher than the last one. That's a big win but only a miniscule one when compared to what The Principle of Completion is targeting.

- Online social and search platforms show us advertisements based on our browsing history and the data companies have managed to dig up about us. Our click probability is still a statistic. They probably have no idea why we click to buy when we do. They do know that a certain percentage of a certain type of online visitors click through to a particular item, and they have certain triggers built in based on analysis of our actions. But do they really know who we are?

What's missing here is a relationship with the customer that is based on the customer's need *behind* their obvious actions. The difference in the new approach of the Principle of Completion is that instead of analyzing the actions, and deriving correlations, we now analyze customer needs and create an appropriate experience, based on actual knowledge of context.

Thinking about products that don't fit our core portfolio seems a little counterintuitive. However, in this digitally connected world, being customer- centric means exactly that.

Significant monetary time and investment are often needed to develop a channel or an offering to the point that it becomes viable in the eyes of the customer. The most complete ecosystem will win the race for customer interest. An ecosystem of interacting entities will allow the building of context which will in turn drive the customer experience. Therefore, a vision for which partners we may need, and how our individual business models will complement and boost each other must be developed. That vision should translate to an incremental roadmap with an eye on the competition and evolving trends.

2. Define the Chain of Links for the Optimal Customer Experience

Even though the traditional business world is segregated by industries, products and domains, the truth is that today's customer experience is increasingly cross-industry. It's not that customers have inherently changed, but it's because new possibilities are now being discovered through emerging technology capabilities.

A few years ago when digital technologies were still emerging, it was expected that a person following the Weight Watchers weight loss plan would go shopping in the grocery aisles, look up calorie counts and compare them with their allowance on their Weight Watcher's plan. It was a manual process. People took notes, carried reference cards and made the mathematical comparisons to keep calories in check. Today, the rise of digital technology allows the same customer to be enabled through mobile and bar code scanning. Customer preferences haven't changed. On the other hand customers have been empowered to do things in different ways which in turn is placing extreme demands on businesses to be much more responsive and agile in their approach to win and retain customers. More and more cross industry use cases are being leveraged today.

- A recent innovation by a Russian bank now awards loyalty rewards to customers based on achievement of their fitness goals. As customers engage in fitness activity, data from their devices such as Fitbit and others are used to calculate the amount of exercise completed that is then transferred to a higher interest account opened by the same customers. This was an excellent use of technology for boosting customer engagement.

There are numerous innovations that are potentially on the horizon. In the end an interconnected, dynamic ecosystem can be created that enables all parties to leverage the same, underlying business and customer data, providing unprecedented, contextual and an effortless customer experience.

- Restaurants leveraging their loyalty card data to help customers maintain their diet plan.

- This can then be leveraged by insurance companies to manage their underwriting risk and pass along the benefits to customers.

- This chain can further be extended by fitness centers working with grocery stores to update the consumers' profile, and then feeding this back to restaurants and insurance firms.

- Banks can then step in to enable seamless payments across the value chain. Their data can be used by financial advisors to help the customers plan their retirement goals.

This seems like a frightening proposition. What about customer privacy? Are customers really going to buy in to this value cycle? Customer surveys are increasingly showing that customers are willing to share their information if they see value in return of such an exchange. This is already happening in a very disjointed manner. Consumers are already providing their data on so many channels and mediums right from social networks to loyalty platforms. Their transaction data in an online world is increasingly available to retailers and their service providers. Rental car companies, logistics carriers, coffee shops – the trail of information is easy to piece together. There are so many independent providers of data and services that the risk can only be reduced by a more controlled ecosystem. Towards that end a conscious development of such an alliance of companies can only benefit the customer privacy concerns. Although proper controls around privacy and consumer consent will always be factors to battle, there is no doubt that this is the direction in which the world is moving.

The keynote speeches in early 2014 by Mark Benioff, Founder and CEO of Salesforce.com, were highlighting similar principles. He used the example of how his toothbrush, by being connected to the Internet, can transmit information that can be used by his dentist in planning his treatments. Although this was more on how the Internet of Things will drive business going forward, he used the term Internet of Customers to allude to the things to come.

The Chain of Links in the customer experience is not limited to consumer- oriented businesses alone. Business to business sales and marketing works on similar principles. The Principle of Completion is also about the Internet of Companies, if you will.

Some typical scenarios for business to business interaction could be:

- Manufacturers of goods can use sensors to track their inventory levels at outlet stores and create unimaginable efficiencies in their supply chains. A repair and service network can also be planned based on this information.

- Chief Information Officers should be thinking of their technology landscape as an inter-connected machine. In this scenario, investments in data, middleware, applications and infrastructure should be made not in isolation, but with an eye on the overall vision of how the various technology machines will work in tandem to enable the business vision – across businesses, across geographies and across customer segments. That's the holy grail of technology. Different software product and services companies should be thinking of working together, not independently.

- Online travel sites allow us to select an origin, destination and date and look for flights and hotels. Do they know why and what we are looking for? We select dates several times to find the best price, and they oblige us by showing us the best prices. It's a zero sum game they are willing to play as per their current business model. Some excellent innovations have been aligned with the Principle of Un-Commoditization as Southwest Airlines found the short trip opportunity, and JetBlue found the customer service and comfort niche. But is the entire travel and hospitality sector ripe for an overhaul of the business model? Could the participating companies put together a better overall package for us by working together across our travel needs right from idea to completion?

- Including customers into the mix is an innovation that The Four Seasons has recently launched. The hotel staff helps the customers plan their itinerary using various social media mechanisms (specifically Pinterest). We can be sure that the model will be extended to local businesses and travel and tourism sites, as well.

To define our ecosystem, the first step is to understand the Chain of Links in the customer experience journey. In my opinion the complexity lies not in identifying the partnerships but in modeling a business plan and roadmap around the Principle of Completion.

3. Build a Scorecard of Results

In the connected economy that is emerging, one of the challenges is in ensuring that potential competitive scenarios are kept in balance. This is true of customer interaction channels as well. We are all aware of the how Borders, a prominent bookseller of the early 2000s, leveraged Amazon as their online commerce partner and in turn lost the race as the e-Commerce model dramatically picked up. A similar story was unfolding for Target before they moved away from Amazon and onto their own ecosystem.

The primary challenge in these specific cases above was the ownership of the customer experience. In both cases the biggest threat that Amazon posed to these two retailers was the ownership of the customer experience and interface. However, the Principle of Completion does not impose that constraint. While specifics will vary, individual companies can maintain their interface with the customer with the added benefit of being immersed into the customer experience of their ecosystem partners.

There are indeed real risks with respect to the merging of business models.

- Consider Amazon and Google. While just a few years ago they seemed to be serving completely different needs, the recent advancements by Amazon have brought them head to head with Google's core search business. Will customers visit Google or

Amazon as they look for products?

- Consider Apple, payment networks like Visa and MasterCard and even banks. With a new payment ecosystem on the iPhone, Apple is now threatening the credit card payment model (or soon may). Indeed, store payment cards like the Target REDcard have already begun to threaten that monopoly as well.

These are scenarios that seem to threaten the future of the business ecosystem. However I argue that these threats seem more real and prominent precisely because businesses haven't thought deeply about the Principle of Completion, and even if they have, they haven't moved rapidly enough. The speed of change in the market is so rapid, and new ideas are coming up so fast that organizational inertia can be fatal. The process of preparing the business cases and implementation plans is often executed at a snail's pace in established businesses. What is needed is a dedicated task force with direct access to the market.

As we build a scorecard to measure and monitor the implementation of the Principle of Completion, there will be a mix of traditional and non-traditional metrics.

1. We will measure routine metrics such as attribution to revenue and engagement. Traditionally, we have been most comfortable measuring these parameters so we can optimize our programs and lay our focus on the right areas.

2. We will measure non-routine parameters that are indicators of risk. These would cater to possession of customer attention and changes in customer interaction. Although they may not provide meaningful information when measured in isolation, we must measure their impact on key parameters such as origin of

customer acquisitions, business transactions and routine operational transactions. While an increase in acquisitions is a

3. good thing, loss of customer interaction may not be. This will of course vary by the specific arrangement of the ecosystem. For example, even how we channel our promotional coupons

4. Finally, we will measure the very important metric of changing business models. Is the interaction model we had envisioned under threat? Is a partner evolving to become an intended or unintended competitor? For example, grocery chains may be seeing increased sales through partners such as providers of make-at-home meals. Are grocery chains also losing the race for customer share of mind? And how does this trend affect restaurants?

Table 6: A sample scorecard to measure and monitor the implementation of The Principle of Completion

Category	What is measured
Routine Metrics	• Attribution to revenue • Attribution to new customer acquisitions
Risk metrics	• Customer attention • Customer interaction
Business model risk	• Partner to competitor migration

As we will see, the ultimate risk in all scenarios is losing the race for the customer experience and being relegated to a back office or as a commodity provider of the required service. That is the primary risk in today's digitally connected economy. The Principle of Completion can alleviate that risk, but it must still always be on the top of your mind.

4. Create a Channel and Medium Roadmap

The biggest risk in any partnership, including those in the Chain of Links created by the Principle of Completion, is of improperly controlling the customer attention and interaction mediums. As we saw in the Principle of Customer Interaction, firms that have a low or medium Customer Interaction Index – those that operate more at the emotional end of the spectrum – have a lot to gain by getting involved in partnership with a partner that has a strong Customer Interaction Index or that operates actively at the physical interaction end of the spectrum.

- The partnership between Wal-Mart and American Express Bluebird is an example of a traditional kind of a partnership that leverages the channel and reach that Wal-Mart has to offer, in turn providing customer stickiness advantages to Wal-Mart. It seems to be a great win for American Express and has extended its physical reach dramatically. This partnership may also allow Wal-Mart to reach more customers, especially those not currently in the banking ecosystem.

A channel and medium roadmap has to do with two primary aspects:

The first consideration is about extending the Chain of Links. Every partnership, in my view, is about improving the breadth of services and creating a unified, seamless customer experience. Business strategy and objectives will dictate whether the progression of the Chain of Links will be towards becoming a conglomerate or towards an ecosystem.

- Wal-Mart can look to be a bank, or it can partner with local credit unions and community banks.

- In turn, other industry players can join in. viz. book sellers, fitness centers, dieticians, soccer coaches etc.

It's a fine line to walk. On one hand, we can give up control too easily, and on the other we can be Big Brother trying to control the ecosystem. Both approaches will fail. The Chain of Links is successful when every player does their part, and benefits tremendously from a connected ecosystem.

The second and complementary step in building out the roadmap is thinking about how to participate in the customer interaction spectrum. Every participant already has a medium through which they interact with their customers. The Chain of Links, through the Principle of Completion, provides an effective avenue to embed ourselves in the interaction spectrum of the other partners in the ecosystem.

- A retailer may provide access to a local bookstore leveraging interactive technology such as kiosks and tablets, and even online over smartphones, wearable devices and the good, old fashioned tablets or laptops
- A bookstore may provide access to a dietician through their health section, who in turn may direct the customers back to the retailer or to a fitness provider as part of diet planning
- An airline or a tourist destination may provide advice based on what the customer is reading about or has as part of their wish list

Trying to extend the spectrum of interactions must mesh effectively with customer privacy concerns. At every interaction point, customer consent must be foremost. The dimensions of consent will be at various levels including access, purpose, persistence and timing.

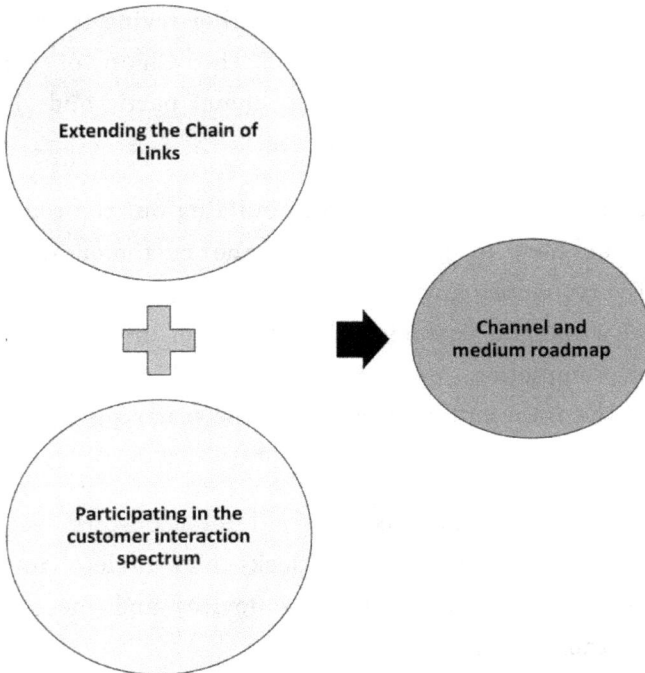

Figure 29: Components of the channel and medium roadmap

- Who will be able to see which pieces of information?
- What will they be able to use it for – in person interaction, sending coupons, sales transactions and many others?
- How persistent is the underlying data? Can it be stored for future use or should it be accessed every time?
- Timing will determine whether we will ask the customer to access their data every time or if we will store the consent for a

set period of time until the need for another business decision
arises

The Reversible Nature of the Chain of Links

An interesting fact about building out the Chain of Links is that it should be thought of as completely reversible. Customers can start from one end of the chain and reach the other in no particular order. In fact, I should call it a web of links because the customer experience can take numerous paths through this Chain of Links.

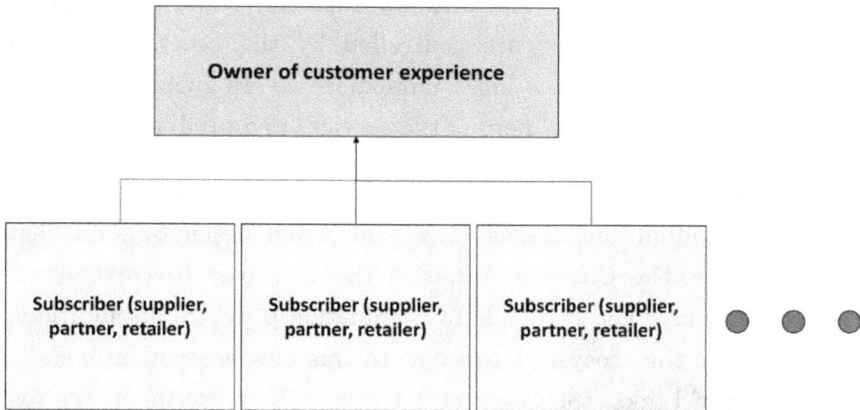

Figure 30: What a traditional ecosystem looks like

Contrast this with the current ecosystems of which we are aware. All of them have a master-slave or a provider-subscriber relationship. Due to this fact, implementing The Principle of Completion may actually mitigate individual business risks about customer attention and interaction. As customers interact with the various links, they are presented with contextual and targeted information. This phenomenon enables a seamless experience across the participants of the ecosystem.

- In the Amazon ecosystem, the primary point of entry is its website or through one of their products such as Kindle.

Individual participants can try to reverse it but it's tough because the market place is owned by Amazon.

- Similarly, in the Apple or Google ecosystem, individual participants must adhere to the host's standards, or be left out.

This is not necessarily wrong. This model also works really well. In the Apple and Google apps ecosystems, individual apps control the customer experience and the result is that ecosystem is closer to the Principle of Completion. The primary customer experience and the terms of the agreement are controlled by the ecosystem owner. Participants can influence more immediate levers such as customer service, shipping or fulfillment of the services and products.

In the new model, no single entity is the master. Of course, this is a choice individual businesses may still make depending on their priorities but the Chain of Links is the new way to traverse the digital economy. The Principle of Completion provides an additional dimension to the ecosystem concept. In this new ecosystem model of the Chain of Links, there are no owners, only subscribers. It's just examining the ecosystem from a new perspective. The only common entity would be a possible backbone provider – or the connector - who would be competing with several other backbone providers – much like Visa and MasterCard, and even the Apple, Google and Amazon app stores. From that perspective the Google and Apple app ecosystems may serve to be that backbone provider. In this scenario, individual apps or businesses are free to strike relationships with any other entity and determine the customer experience across the chain of links. The only difference is that these present day networks are sponsored by specific organizations so they are not a true manifestation of the Principle of Completion. However it's a giant evolution from the options available just a few years ago.

The Chain of Links will be formed as the extent of customer interactions evolves and as businesses explore opportunities to navigate the web of customer experience. Customers can enter the ecosystem from any point, and the only evidence of the ecosystem is the ease of transactions across the participants.

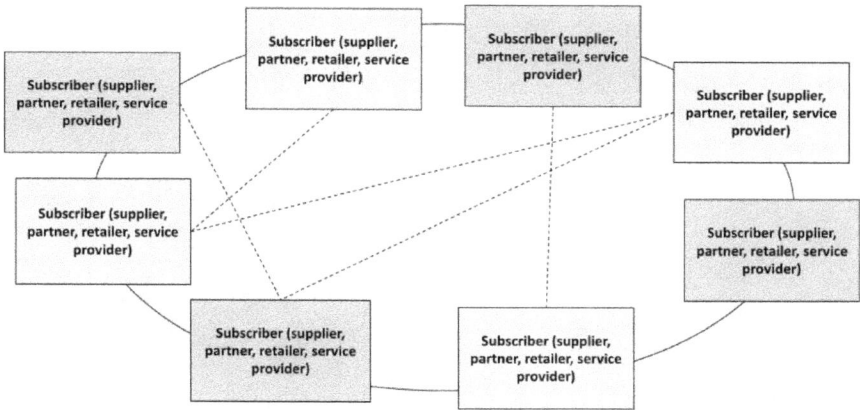

Figure 31: The Chain of Links

The Infinite Nature of the Chain of Links

By infinite, I do not mean the number of participants. That is infinite in any ecosystem. I mean infinite in that the participants open themselves up to an infinite array of customer experience scenario and are not limited by the purpose or infrastructure of the ecosystem that is owned by one participant. For example Amazon is restricted to retail sales and Apple is restricted to the technology landscape they provide.

The types of scenarios possible are only limited by imagination. And we know that there is no shortage of that in this world. Just like the Russian bank created a dedicated savings account based on the fitness habits and accomplishments of its customers, businesses of all kinds can create rewarding and unique customer experiences. The primary examination that is needed is that of looking closely at the value chain and figuring out where we can fit in our own value proposition.

- Firms like DinnerThyme, Plated, Blue Apron are creating menus and delivering pre-packed ingredients directly to consumers. What partnerships can we uncover here? Perhaps dinner preparation videos, chefs, dieticians, menu discovery, having fun with recipes, fitness calculators, restaurants, grocery chains, shipping companies, environmental impact calculators, and coffee shops. There are so many possibilities.

- Chains such as Panera and Chipotle are operating independently today. Could services like Blue Apron and DinnerThyme offer meals that complement what I had for lunch at Panera today? Can grocery supermarkets manage their inventory better given this information?
- There are machines to check our blood pressure and heart rate at

many supermarkets today. What kind of ecosystem can you imagine here?

The sky is the limit when it comes to uncovering links. What's needed is the destruction of walls that exist between businesses.

Consider business to business scenarios. Can cloud and infrastructure services providers deliver the links between businesses themselves? We all try to sell to businesses by saying we understand their end customers. But we lose ourselves in the products of that specific client, and in the nitty-gritty of their technology infrastructure complexities. In the new Chain of Links approach, perhaps we could help them discover and achieve the potential of cross-industry collaboration and use cases that help the client embed their products into the overall needs spectrum of their customers.

- Will we allow CRM platforms like Salesforce.com to look into the client information and automatically present service providers? Or better yet, can a third party app on Salesforce.com make this inquiry and connect a user of Salesforce.com to a client with a completely different CRM platform such as Microsoft Dynamics?

- Can a marketing services provider who runs campaigns to consumers like us, be able to package complementary services from multiple clients and send a more coherent and lucrative offer to a consumer? For example, I'd love to see promotions from Starbucks and Banana Republic in the same package for the same Mall, so the allure of going to the Mall is doubled!

This is a radically different approach and one that could allow infrastructure providers to be the orchestrators of critical business communications.

The Chain of Links does not imply that we somehow need a magical technology layer that connects these businesses together. We already have the needed technology in the form of the Internet, Facebook, Whatapp, Instagram, Twitter, Pinterest, Google, and many other such platforms. All we need is a change in mindset so the customers look at these as extensions of our business. When we begin to think like that, the horizons are limitless. The Internet of Things phenomenon is making devices intelligent, or at least capable of receiving and transmitting data. This implies that we do not need a human at the other end to feed the interaction.

The Customer as Master, and Sometimes - Almost

As seen from the diagram of the Chain of Links, participants control the way their relationship are built as per the Principle of Completion. And participants in turn are controlled by the way customers would like their own individual relationships to develop.

The Chain of Links provides an additional way for innovation to be executed. And the method is guided by the customers, and how the innovation makes it easier, or more difficult or more profitable for them.

The chain of links will be built over time as methods to meet the overall customer experience are discovered. Customers will determine the fate of many such initiatives but it is important to note that sometimes, initiatives fail because we are just not ready for them. Often, one or more ingredient is missing in the overall scheme of things. These missing ingredients make it difficult to achieve the intended purpose. And when the ingredient is finally added, a new and better way for meeting the same need is discovered. Online grocery shopping and delivery surfaced dramatically late in the dot com boom, and then died down until recently when successes were discovered in the UK for Tesco and in the US with Amazon. Finally, online shopping lists and delivery services like Peapod are picking up.

Sometimes, customer perceptions and slow adoption take time to work themselves out. Unlike the iPod and the iPhone which took off so fast that entrenched competitors had no time to respond, many models take time to play themselves out. Customers rely on other customers for feedback and then the adoption curve accelerates. Blockbuster and Circuit City perished relatively slowly given the time scales we are used to now. And the entire publishing and news industry has fortunately had time to reinvent itself, a little.

Sometimes, customers must be made to compete for resources to really drive adoption. Scarcity and exclusivity are known drivers of demand, and they can make customers want something different that is actually similar to what they already have. This could have been why Facebook triumphed so comprehensively. The momentum created by the initial demand snowballed into a revolution, with the rapid innovation being a contributor, of course.

The Chain of Links will always be guided by the customer, and the customers will always follow the promise and delivery of exceptional experience and value. It's always a tradeoff between convenience, excitement and the costs associated with it. Would customers want their restaurant lunches to factor automatically into their fitness plan and vice versa? That's probably a resounding yes. Would they want their fitness information shared with third party marketers bombarding them with promotions? That's not likely. Innovations using the Principle of Completion will be counter-balanced by the customers themselves.

Summary – The Principle of Completion

Today's dizzying pace of business in the digital world will require us to innovate with the customer experience in mind.

The Principle of Completion is different from other published views about cross-industry partnerships. So far, these have been focused around either software ecosystems like Apple's, or Amazon, which is bringing suppliers and partners together from related industries for the purposes of supporting their core business model. The principle I've laid out in this chapter is centered on creating a customer experience that transcends industries altogether. No one is in charge and yet everyone is in charge. Does a continuous evolution of this manner threaten or dilute brand identity? Not if we follow the Principle of Completion rather than trying to become new things to new customers. Evolution brings to light new possibilities in normal customer interaction. And completing ourselves with capabilities from different industries is the key.

Let's try the following exercise:

- Draw a simple diagram of our customer's value chain. Pick any one customer type.
- Circle the parts where we fit in.
- Now try to draw arrows around our circle by listing actions that our customers are performing before, during and after they use our services (or those of our direct competition) to get the job done.

Once we are done, we will be staring at the adjacencies in our model that are threats to our business.

Conclusion

As the customer engagement fabric is being built in the marketplace, we should define and build in entry points to our own businesses. The five principles are interlinked in many different ways and feed into each other.

More than customers, we ourselves are set in our way and the ways of how our industry works. The Principle of Completion through its chain of links provides a framework through which to view our industry through the eyes of the customer.

Unfortunately, fear is a great motivator. There is always a fear of the unknown. There are multi-trillion dollar industries based on fear – and how the participants address the privacy and security concerns will define how the ecosystem evolves. However, the biggest risk is in not formulating a strategy in response to the rapidly innovating digital world. If we innovate too quickly, we'll lose the race at the emotional end of the customer interaction spectrum. If we're too slow, someone else will replace us at the physical end of the spectrum.

Incremental innovations and operational efficiency may keep a business afloat, but there are no guarantees in today's world. The only way to stay ahead is to revisit our customer experience strategies and traverse the entire customer experience path. And as we do that, the methods should transcend our industries, our products and our services. Because as we discovered through The Principle of Presenting and The Principle of Completion, the customer needs spectrum is much better organized than what we and our partners may offer and imagine.

We discussed earlier in the book how organizational culture is influenced in a big way by how we view the market. The ability to continuously innovate and push the boundaries of customer experience depends a great deal on how we view our own organization. Customers constantly send signals about how they would like to interact with us. An organization that is solely looking at its own products and services will struggle to evolve rapidly enough. The new world is about creating a partnership with customers and about meeting their needs. Our culture should be nurtured from that perspective.

We all have ideas, and I myself have taken the liberty of imagining fantastic customer experience scenarios in this book. Some of them may appear to be far-fetched, but the only person really in-charge of that decision is the customer. And sometimes customers need to be shown the possibilities before they come on board. We all know the story of Henry Ford and his assembly line for Model T, but there are more recent examples:

- For almost a decade, phone, music player and camera manufacturers innovated and launched new models, often with exciting capabilities. But it took Steve Jobs to define the essence of how the consumer experience should be and the rest is history.

- When Netflix started operating it took some time before we understood the magnitude of disruption. That inertia in reengineering the video rental business spelled doom for the established business models.

- As Amazon quietly operated, all eyes were on the rival booksellers. Now Amazon has taken the publishing industry by storm, is disrupting Netflix, the online search business and perhaps even how we search and shop for everything.

- The hospitality industry is now realizing the significance and power of the peer-peer model.

- The CRM software industry is rapidly taking over the front end of all enterprise business units. No user is unaffected. Who would have imagined that what was considered a sales and service software would become the centerpiece of our customer experience strategy?

Examples are all around us if we only take the time to question our business models in this emerging digital world. We must constantly push the boundaries of our existence and keep an eye on the purpose for which we exist. It has been said numerous times before that a business model or products and services portfolio is not the purpose of a company. Only in the fast paced, connected world of today is that phrase ringing truer than ever. A relentless focus on our purpose will help us be the innovative and flexible enterprise that we aspire to be.

Customer needs are intricately linked with the services and products of many other industry players. No longer are decisions made in the absence of information. And when they are, the victories are short lived, or painful to cherish. Even as we win, we must reinforce our customers' choices in light of all the other choices they could have made. The Principle of External Reinforcement shows how the traditional model of promoting our own products is woefully inadequate, and results in yielding control of the customer experience to others who may not do justice to the merit of our products. The key to avoid that is to become the reference point for our customers. And the only way to accomplish that is to be a true partner as customers decide what's right for them.

We can address aspects of each of the five principles in any order based on where we are in our journey. But it is important to make progress on each of these at all times. They all feed into each other.

- We cannot bring together the physical and emotional ends of the customer interaction spectrum unless we are also looking at how we cater to the Principle of External Reinforcement.

- Doing so will require us to revisit The Principle of Un-

Commoditization to ensure that we are devising the right messages and evolving our organization in the right direction.

- While we think about that, it will be necessary to consider how we are tying all of our services together to bring them to meet the linked customer needs. That's The Principle of Presenting. Integrating our products and services is crucial to energizing the organization so that all engines fire in tandem.

- And lastly, all of this must take into account The Principle of Completion to continuously evaluate how we are partnering with companies that apparently have little to do with our own existence.

However much we try to isolate ourselves, the fact remains that the real battle is for customer engagement. As the customer engagement fabric is being built in the marketplace, we should define and build in entry points to our own businesses. This perspective also implies that the quest for deep customer engagement is not only about our channels, but about everything else that makes the channels click – operational processes, technology, costs, people, partnerships and customer service among many other capabilities. In fact we can even term this overall strategy as ecosystem marketing.

The Five Principles presented in *Dancing The Digital Tune: The 5 Principles of Competing in a Digital World* provide a sound framework and a systematic process for assessing how to best compete in a digital world.

Good luck!